Decision Making

Originally published in 1968, Richard Chapman's pioneering work illuminates the process of decision making by analysis of a particular example: the decision to raise the Bank Rate in Sep tember, 1957. The legal responsibility for a decision may be easy to pinpoint; in this case the Court of Directors of the Bank of England bear this but six weeks of negotiation separate their formal statement from the Chancellor of the Exchequer's advice to the Treasury to consider effecting 'a measure of deflation in the economy'. These six weeks of consultation between the Bank and the Treasury proceeding in 'the pattern of a formal dance' are analysed and a necessary by product of this case study is a closer understanding of how the Treasury and the Bank of England work together. These details are derived mainly from the evidence, and deductions from it, presented to the Bank Rate Tribunal and the Radcliffe Committee on the Working of the Monetary System.

Professor Chapman gives his particular findings about decision making a wider application still by forming reasoned hypotheses and informed generalisations about public administration in Brit ain.

'**Mr Chapman's case study is a pioneering work. He looks at how and why the decision was reached and gives an exciting reconstruction of how the decision was taken**' *The Times*

Decision Making

A case study of the decision to raise
the Bank Rate in September 1957

Richard A. Chapman

Routledge
Taylor & Francis Group

First published in 1968
by Routledge & Kegan Paul Ltd

This edition first published in 2011 by Routledge
2 Park Square, Milton Park, Abingdon, Oxon, OX14 4RN

Simultaneously published in the USA and Canada
by Routledge
711 Third Avenue, New York, NY 10017

Routledge is an imprint of the Taylor & Francis Group, an informa business

Publisher's Note
The publisher has gone to great lengths to ensure the quality of this
reprint but points out that some imperfections in the original copies may
be apparent.

Disclaimer
The publisher has made every effort to trace copyright holders and
welcomes correspondence from those they have been unable to contact.

A Library of Congress record exists under ISBN: 0710063024

ISBN 13: 978-0-415-50817-9 (hbk)
ISBN 13: 978-0-203-12569-4 (ebk)

Decision Making

A case study of the decision to raise
the Bank Rate in September 1957

by Richard A. Chapman

Reader in Politics
University of Durham

LONDON

ROUTLEDGE & KEGAN PAUL
NEW YORK: HUMANITIES PRESS

First published 1968
by Routledge & Kegan Paul Ltd
Broadway House, 68-74 Carter Lane
London, EC4V 5EL
Reprinted 1971

Printed in Great Britain
by Unwin Brothers Limited
The Gresham Press, Old Woking, Surrey

ISBN 0 7100 7226 0 (p)
ISBN 0 7100 6302 4 (c)

General editor's introduction

This series of monographs is designed primarily to meet the needs of students of government, politics, or political science in Universities and other institutions providing courses leading to degrees. Each volume aims to provide a brief general introduction indicating the significance of its topic, e.g. executives, parties, pressure groups, etc., and then a longer 'case study' relevant to the general topic. First year students will thus be introduced to the kind of detailed work on which all generalisations must be based, while more mature students will have an opportunity to become acquainted with recent original research in a variety of fields. The series will eventually provide a comprehensive coverage of most aspects of political science in a more interesting and fundamental manner than in the large volume which often fails to compensate by breadth what it inevitably lacks in depth.

There are few case studies of how administrators go about their work, at least on this side of the Atlantic, and this monograph is one of the pioneering studies in this field. The volume is concerned with an analysis of the decision to raise the Bank Rate in September, 1957. It presents a considerable amount of evidence shedding light on how the Bank of England and the Treasury work together. These details are derived mainly from the evidence, and deductions from it, presented to the Bank Rate Tribunal and the Radcliffe Committee on the Working of the Monetary System. In his discussion and analysis of decision-making in this particular context, Mr Chapman uses his material as the basis of hypotheses about public administration in general.

An article on this subject by Mr Chapman appeared in *Public Administration*, Summer 1965, Vol. 43 and we are grateful to the Editor for permission to make use of this.

H.V.W.

Contents

1
Introduction

'An executive decision is a moment in a process. The growth of a decision, the accumulation of authority, not the final step, is what we need most to study.'
(Follett, 1949, 1.)

Students of public administration in Britain need to consider how administrators really work. It is not very valuable to know merely what institutions *are*, we must also know what they *do*. Professor W. A. Robson has said, 'few studies have appeared showing how government departments really do their work—I can say this after having read all the volumes of *The New Whitehall Series*' (*Public Administration*, 1961). And the Editor of *Public Law*, after recalling Robson's remarks, has commented that there are no books on administrative law which approach the subject through 'the administrative process', by showing the way in which decisions are taken and the political and legal forces which have shaped those decisions (*Public Law*, 1961).

However, it is easier to notice this sort of gap in the study of public administration than to fill it. This is partly because it is difficult to make any detailed study of how government departments work without willing co-operation from the departments concerned. It is also partly because the descriptive method favoured by most British writers on public administration has not been adequate for this purpose. While factual description may illustrate some aspects of how administrators work, this alone may not be

1

very penetrating. We need to be able to evaluate the facts in order to decide which are the most important; we need also to examine the motives of the administrators and the forces which influence their actions. In order to discover how government departments really do their work theory and facts have to be considered together—a hypothesis is formulated, the facts examined and the hypothesis may be modified and retested against further facts. If the facts are presented on their own the result may be formal and un-real; it may be argued, for example, that the lack of theoretical discussion is the main weakness of both *The New Whitehall Series* of studies of government depart-ments and of *Administrators in Action*, the two volumes of case studies sponsored by the Royal Institute of Public Administration.

This present study began with the disbelief that the pro-cedure for making a decision to raise the Bank Rate was as simple as appeared from statements in the House of Commons and in the Report of the Bank Rate Tribunal. The disbelief was aggravated by the explanations given to the Tribunal, of how the decision was made on Septem-ber 19th 1957. The formal statements and explanations seemed unreal compared with the other evidence given before the Bank Rate Tribunal. This provided the basis on which the facts have been collected and presented with critical discussion.

Although more work has been done in this field of study in the United States, American knowledge does not greatly help to fill the gap in British public administration. This is partly because of the different systems of government in the two countries, but it is also because of the different attitudes held by American and British students of public administration. The American school has largely turned away from the institutional aspects of government and has concentrated more on the informal and psychological relationships within and between administrative organisations. This difference is reflected in the different attitudes to the study of decision-making. Whilst in America the study of decision-making has become a respectable academic pursuit, in Britain this area of study has been almost confined to the reflections and recollections of practising administrators. For example, the American writers Richard C. Snyder and Glenn D. Paige have said (*Administrative Science Quarterly*, 1958-9) 'decision-making is a sequence of activities which results in selection of one course of action intended to bring about the particular future state of affairs envisaged by the decision-makers'. On the other hand, Sir David Kelly might be regarded as an example of the British attitude in his observation that decision-making is frequently 'casual unreasoning action by ordinary men in positions of extraordinary power (Kelly, 1952, 1). Not only are American students of government more inclined to use concepts from the other social sciences, the attitudes of the administrators themselves are also more influenced by these disciplines which are still more highly regarded in the United States than they are in Britain.

The main purpose of this essay is therefore to contribute to our knowledge of how institutions work by studying how they worked on one particular occasion—the decision to raise the Bank Rate by two per cent on September 19th 1957. The study involves not only a gathering together of the details of what happened at that particular time but also an examination of their significance.

It is comparatively easy to see that a decision has been made when there is an obvious change in direction of policy. But it is often difficult to see exactly who made the decision, when the process began which resulted in its formulation, and when it ended. It may be very easy to

3

say that the Bank Rate rose from five per cent to seven per cent on September 19th, and to note who was legally responsible for making the decision (the Court of Directors of the Bank of England). But that does not account for the fact that it took six weeks from August 7th, when the Chancellor of the Exchequer left instructions for the Treasury to consider the possibility of 'bringing about a measure of deflation in the economy', to the date when the Bank Rate was actually raised. During those weeks holidays caused delays but the monetary situation continued to be watched very closely by the Bank, and consultations proceeded between the Bank and the Treasury in what *The Economist* (5 January 1958) has called 'the pattern of a formal dance'.

The Prime Minister had an important role to play in the decision; as executive head of the government he sanctioned the decision. But much is contributed to an executive decision of government before the part which the executive head takes in it—which in many cases is only the official promulgation of the decision. There is a need to study the growth of the decision, how the authority was accumulated, rather than just the final step, the formulation of the decision.

Whilst it may be interesting to see who makes the final formulation, the important thing about a decision is not so much who makes it as what goes into it. Government decisions are rarely made by individuals in isolation. In our system of government they are usually made by groups of people who each have interests and who react on each other. Furthermore, the decision-makers are rarely dealing with constant facts. In government, the facts of any problem may change from day to day or even from hour to hour. In one sense it could therefore be argued that the whole process of decision-making in British government is

4

really a matter of people gathering and discussing the facts of the situation and deciding which facts are relevant.

In this essay it is not intended to rake over the embers of an almost dead party political controversy. Nor is it intended to attack the officials or politicians concerned. The intention is to find out, and discuss, significant features about how they worked on this particular occasion, the raising of the Bank Rate on September 19th 1957.

Apart from the fact that this is an uncommon exercise in British public administration there are other difficulties, of which the main one is that the student is faced with a combination of the doctrine of ministerial responsibility and the inaccessibility of material which is controlled by the Public Records Act, 1967.

Professor H. W. R. Wade has observed that 'convention forbids any inquiry as to who has advised ministers or what advice has been given (Wade, 1961, 16). Two arguments are sometimes heard in favour of this convention. First, if it was possible for such advice to be published this may affect the nature of the officials' advice, or even inhibit them from giving any advice at all. Secondly, the present system enables civil servants to work in an atmosphere of detachment and to give their services to a government of any complexion with impartiality. But these arguments may not be as valid as they at first appear. In the first place, publication of such advice may lead to greater care in its preparation and presentation and this could benefit government. And if the advice was subsequently criticised it does not seem unreasonable that the civil servants and advisers should be permitted to defend themselves publicly (after all, we already know *who* they are even if we do not know the exact advice they gave or how they gave it, and the officials themselves may welcome the opportunity to defend themselves). Secondly, it

5

may be time to set aside the fiction that officials are a class of disinterested mandarin-like creatures. As Professor Brian Chapman has said, 'Nobody really believes that senior civil servants are faceless, pliable, sexless creatures without fixed ideas, or intellectual eunuchs impartially proffering advice with all deference and humility to the great man in the minister's office' (Chapman, 1963, 39).

In the case of this 1957 decision where we already know so much, it may be argued that disclosing *how* the advice was given, far from harming the institutions or persons involved, may be beneficial by clearing away ambiguities in the public mind about a public corporation that has notoriously neglected public relations. However, all requests to see the statements taken by the Treasury Solicitor on behalf of the Tribunal have been refused, although the Treasury Solicitor has intimated that these records will be available for public inspection in the year 1987.

It is not surprising, therefore, that there are a number of gaps in our knowledge. For example, the Prime Minister had an important role in the making of this decision and must surely have given the problem much more thought than is revealed in the Minutes of Evidence taken before the Bank Rate Tribunal. The decision to raise the Bank Rate was delayed until the Governor of the Bank of England returned from his holiday (though the Deputy Governor had full power to act in his absence); and it would be useful to know why it was necessary to wait for the Governor, also, assuming the Governor's presence was vital, whether he was not recalled from holiday because the publicity that may have been attracted might have had a worsening effect on the situation.

Such gaps in our knowledge as these must be remembered when reading the case study. The reason for them is that the case study has been based on the published

6

Evidence of a Tribunal of Inquiry that was not primarily concerned with how the decision was made. And only evidence relevant to the purpose of the inquiry has been published.

The plan of the essay is first to describe the background to the decision. Since the system itself is a factor in the decision-making, 'the background' includes an explanation of the legal position, how the institutions involved are expected to work together, and details of who was responsible in accordance with the provisions of the Bank of England Act, 1946. It also includes an account of the economic situation in the summer of 1957. This chapter therefore covers some of the institutional aspects, but it is brief because the purpose of the essay is to concentrate on how the people involved went about their tasks on this particular occasion. What *should* happen may be important, but it is often more important to know what *does* happen and *why*.

This is followed by a chronological, descriptive reconstruction, with as much detail as possible, of the decision-making activities leading up to the pronouncement of the change in the Bank Rate on September 19th. This method of concentrating on one particular decision, or 'depth' study of a single case, is adopted because it has distinct advantages. Little published work has been done in this way in Britain and no-one can learn what data can be thrown away until he has some idea what the sum total of data is like. Also, as Arthur Bentley has observed, many a child making paper toys has used his scissors too confidently and cut himself off from the materials he needs (Bentley, 1908, 199).

This approach means, however, that there are really two fields of inquiry in the essay. There are the facts of the decision (including the absence of certain evidence con-

7

cerning those facts), and the measuring of those facts against theoretical considerations, and developing theory from the facts.

In such a case study as this there is a tendency to regard some features as unusual, or peculiar in relation to some vaguer, more conventional 'governmental process'. It may for example, be argued that the raising of the Bank Rate by two per cent on this occasion was so unusual that anything we learn from the case should be qualified by the peculiar circumstances. On the other hand, it may be more useful to recognise that every problem and every decision in public administration is peculiar. There is no one, obvious, accepted, 'governmental process' to which all specific cases conform.

However, whilst it is indeed rare for a Tribunal to provide the student with so much information about how government works, raising the Bank Rate from five per cent to seven per cent is not, in itself, unique. The Bank Rate also rose to seven per cent in November 1907, August 1914 and April 1920. In more recent years, the increases on July 25th 1961 and November 23rd 1964 were again from five per cent to seven per cent (and on November 18th 1967 the increase was from six and a half per cent to eight per cent). This has now led some observers to generalise that raising the Bank Rate to seven per cent is an almost routine procedure at a time of economic crisis. Samuel Brittan, for example, writes of 'the testing point for every Chancellor . . . during his first big sterling crisis when he must choose between slamming down the brakes (usually signalled by a seven per cent Bank Rate) and breaking with established orthodoxy' (Brittan, 1964, 252).

Although the method of studying a single case has limitations, it also has advantages. Any study of decision-making in British government has to start somewhere, and until the field work has been done it is difficult to produce answers, or even suggestions, to questions that face students of public administration. Such questions are: Why do decision-makers behave as they do? What are the possible effects of the decision-maker's social conditioning *before* he takes office? Where and how do the decision-makers get their ideas? Does the decision-maker's socio-economic status and previous experience make any difference to the way he looks at policy problems? or in the social groups he will listen to and agree with? Are certain strata of the population over-represented because decision-makers do or do not share their basic characteristics? Are decision-makers recruited from all citizens who have the requisite capacity, or are some excluded? Do the most high ranking social groups dominate the decision-maker roles?

These questions cannot be answered, even tentatively, until we have some clear knowledge of specific cases in public administration. It is for this reason that such a detailed reconstruction is given in Chapters 3 and 4.

The last two chapters are concerned with the development of communications between the Bank of England and the Treasury, the significance of holidays and various other social aspects, particularly the social backgrounds and attitudes of the decision-makers. The aim of these chapters is to contribute to our knowledge of the behaviour of decision-makers and therefore also contribute to a clearer view of how government works.

These aspects of social background also reflect the role of human nature in public administration. Whilst students of organisational behaviour have recognised that rationality is a desirable basis for decision-making, given the nature of man, his organisations and contradictory emotions and

9

needs, they should not assume that rationality is in fact the primary basis of decision-making. There are pressures and influences on decision-makers other than those peculiar to any particular case and those pressures and influences ought also to be considered in the study of decision-making. This means that it is not reasonable to regard administration as 'a universal process', in the way that some writers do. Whilst 'ensuring rational, "efficient" behaviour' (Pfiffner and Presthus, 1960, 3-4) may be accepted as the aim of administration, that aim is not wholly attainable because men cannot be relied upon to act rationally.

The last chapters also contain some theoretical analysis. Marshall E. Dimock has said that the busy executive needs 'a philosophy of administration' because it is the indispensable tool of decision-making and every decision needs to be related to 'an overall strategy which is built on the bedrock of philosophy' (Dimock uses the term philosophy in 'the institutional sense of trying to discover the principles of human action and conduct which promote institutional vitality and the good life', (Dimock, 1968, ch. 1). If this is so, students of government should ask themselves whether the administrators they are studying have such a philosophy, and, if so, what are the main elements of that philosophy? If the decision cannot be related to such a philosophy it may have to be related to something else. Sometimes the alternative may be a set of rules or procedures and this means that the decision-maker may be no more than a cog in a machine or a slave of a system.

Also, students of formal administration, concerned with structure, authority and responsibility, sometimes suppose that a choice is presented to an official as the result of some generally accepted procedure. This procedure, it is supposed, has digested many pressures playing upon the choice and sifted out for the attention of the top administrator those arguments within his prescribed area of discretion. But the decision-maker has to do much more than weigh up two or three possibilities and make a choice. There are sometimes many forces at work on him whilst he is trying to make the decision. And we rarely know what happens to top decision-makers at that time.

Furthermore, democratic theories, if they are to make any sense in government at all, must be as relevant to administrative processes as to political or legislative processes. There must, for example, be some working policy, some rule of thumb, adopted by administrators to deal with the clash between their public and private interests and responsibilities. For a potential clash between public and private interests occurs at almost every point of political or economic decision in a democracy. It affects all M.P.s who also belong to a trade association or trade union, all ministers or civil servants who hold any stocks or shares, indeed anybody who may influence any policy decision who has connections directly or indirectly with any interest and whose attitude of mind may be favourable towards that interest.

It is hoped that this approach will result in a useful contribution to our knowledge of how public administration works. It is a pioneer work, for there has been no other published study made in this way. Most writings on public administration in Britain have followed the formal approach, describing what institutions are; previous case studies have similarly concentrated on the facts and set aside theoretical discussion.

2
Background to the decision and the Tribunal

Although responsibility for varying the Bank Rate rests with the Court of Directors of the Bank of England, 'it is normally—it is always done in consultation with and with the approval of the Chancellor of the Exchequer' (Thorneycroft, *Bank Rate Tribunal Evidence*).

The Bank Rate Tribunal

On September 19th 1957 the Bank Rate was raised from five per cent to seven per cent, the highest figure since 1921. The Chancellor also announced on that day that public investment and bank advances would be held down to the existing level, that banks would intensify the restriction of credit and that the Government intended to maintain the exchange rate of the pound. Following the announcements there were rumours that some persons had known about the impending rise in the Bank Rate before the 19th, and jobbers in the gilt-edged market complained of heavy offerings of Government securities on Wednesday evening, September 18th. When Parliament reassembled, questions were asked in the House of Commons and the Prime Minister and Chancellor of the Exchequer replied that there was no evidence to substantiate the rumours.

When the rumours continued, the Lord Chancellor, at the invitation of the Prime Minister, personally carried out an inquiry lasting ten days and involving interviews with

12

26 persons, into certain allegations that there had been prior disclosure of the decision to increase the Bank Rate. Although the Lord Chancellor had no powers to take evidence on oath or to get records of the sales on the Stock Exchange, he reported to the Prime Minister, and the Prime Minister decided that 'after a most careful and searching inquiry into every aspect of the evidence produced and down every path to which that evidence might lead' (*House of Commons Debates*, 14 November 1957), there was no case for a further inquiry. But the rumours persisted.

Eventually, Labour members of 'the House of Commons asked the Chancellor of the Exchequer questions which implied that he had prematurely disclosed information about the Bank Rate, and which mentioned Mr Oliver Poole (now Lord Poole), then Deputy Chairman of the Conservative party, in connection with the disclosure. Poole wrote to the Prime Minister, denying that there had been any such disclosure to him, either by the Chancellor of the Exchequer, or anyone else, and he asked that a tribunal of inquiry be set up.

The Tribunal that was set up by Mr R. A. Butler (now Lord Butler), then the Home Secretary, on November 14th 1957, to inquire 'whether there is any justification for allegations that information about the raising of the Bank Rate was improperly disclosed to any person, and whether if there was such disclosure any use was made of such information for the purpose of private gain', was appointed in accordance with Section 1 of the Tribunals of Inquiry (Evidence) Act, 1921. This meant that it was set up expressly in accordance with a resolution of both Houses of Parliament 'that a Tribunal be established to inquire into a definite matter of urgent public importance'.

Under the 1921 Act, the Tribunal was armed with full

powers for taking evidence on oath, and it also had the same powers as are vested in the High Court to enforce the attendance of witnesses and compel the production of documents. If any person failed to attend or refused to answer questions, the Chairman of the Tribunal could certify the offence to the High Court, which can hear the alleged offence and has power to punish a person as if he had been guilty of contempt of the Court.

The history of Tribunals of Inquiry is an interesting one, and has already been well written by Professor George W. Keeton in his book *Trial by Tribunal*. The 1957 Bank Rate Tribunal was the thirteenth Tribunal to be set up under the 1921 Act, and it consisted of Lord Justice Parker (now Lord Chief Justice of England), who was appointed Chairman, and two other members, Mr (now Sir) Edward Milner Holland Q.C. and Mr (now Sir) Geoffrey Veale Q.C. The Parker Tribunal decided from the beginning to set aside the Lord Chancellor's inquiry and to make a completely independent investigation. It followed the precedent of its immediate predecessor, the Lynsky Tribunal of 1948, in sitting first of all (on November 21st), at the Royal Courts of Justice to consider procedure and make pertinent arrangements, then from December 2nd it sat at Church House, Westminster, to hear evidence and arguments. In the Report it was stated that the Tribunal heard evidence on oath from 132 witnesses, considered a statutory declaration from one witness, and was also supplied with and considered written statements from 236 other persons.

Though such a Tribunal is in form a Court of Justice it is in substance a fact-finding agency. There is no prosecutor and accused as in a criminal case, and no plaintiff and defendant as in a civil case. It is an Inquiry with no charges and no pleadings. Its report is presented to the Home Secretary and is published by the Stationery Office as an official paper. Because it is a fact-finding agency, a considerable amount of incidental information is received relating to the practice of government: the Minutes of Evidence taken before the Tribunal constitute the main source of information in this examination of how the decision to raise the Bank Rate was made.

The legal responsibility

Subject to any directions which may be given by Her Majesty's Treasury under Section 4, subsection (1), of the Bank of England Act, 1946, the responsibility for fixing the Bank Rate rests with the Court of Directors of the Bank. Section 4 (1) states that 'The Treasury may from time to time give such directions to the Bank as, after consultation with the Governor of the Bank, they think necessary in the public interest' and Section 4 (2) states that 'Subject to any such directions, the affairs of the Bank shall be managed by the Court of Directors in accordance with such provisions (if any) in that behalf as may be contained in any charter of the Bank for the time being in force and any byelaws made thereunder'.

It is further provided in the Act that the Governor, Deputy Governor and the sixteen other members of the Court of Directors are to be appointed by Her Majesty. In practice this is done on the advice of the Prime Minister and the Chancellor of the Exchequer, and Mr C. F. Cobbold (now Lord Cobbold) has explained that during his time as Governor, the Chancellor discussed such matters with him before recommending an appointment. He said this procedure meant that it was 'absolutely unthinkable' that somebody who had not got a record of complete integrity should ever be considered.

The Governor and Deputy Governor are appointed for

15

terms of five years, the directors for terms of four years. Up to four directors, known as executive directors, may be employed full-time on the work of the Bank, the other twelve are part-time directors. All directors attend the weekly meeting of the Court. The Bank's policy committee is a sub-committee of the Court, known as the Committee of Treasury, and it also meets regularly each week. It has seven members, including the Governor, who presides, and the Deputy Governor. Not more than one of the other five members may be an executive director.

The Bank Rate is considered by the Bank of England every week, and the Governor makes a recommendation to the Committee of Treasury each Wednesday morning for approval and for submission to the Court of Directors the next morning, Thursday.

Writing his regular article 'As I See It . . .', in *The Banker* in 1958, Sir Oscar Hobson commented on the Bank's procedure for considering Bank Rate. Hobson recalled that in the 1920s and 1930s three journalists had the entrée to the Bank Parlour. They were Mr Mill of *The Times*, Mr Kiddy of the *Morning Post*, and later Mr Reid of *The Daily Telegraph*, and they made a habit of calling on the Governor each Wednesday, the day before the Governor, after consultation with the members of the Court in the Committee of Treasury, had made up his mind about the following day's Bank Rate decision. It is not known what exchange of views took place at those meetings, but those experienced journalists evolved a code with which to translate the no doubt discreet sentiments that were uttered by the Governor. In those days—that is, before 1932—the Bank Rate changed rather frequently; and by reading between the lines of Mill's column in *The Times* on Thursday, it was possible to form a fairly accurate view of what was going to happen a little before midday. This became apparent to some of the directors who had not been brought into the inner consultative circle and, not unnaturally, they resented reading in *The Times*, *Morning Post*, or *The Daily Telegraph*, oblique but often unmistakable indications of what they were going to decide a few hours later. They registered their protests and some time in the early 1930s Wednesday was made a forbidden day—a *dies non*—for journalists at the Bank.

In the event of a proposed change it is now the normal practice for the Governor to ascertain whether the Chancellor will agree before he makes the proposal to the Committee of Treasury on the Wednesday morning. Although the present procedure (since 1959) is for the Governor to make a formal written proposal to the Chancellor and for the Chancellor to convey to the Governor his formal approval in writing, the legal responsibility for the final decision about a change in the Bank Rate still rests with the Bank's Court of Directors, subject to any directions that may be received (but in this particular case the Governor was given no directions under Section 4 (1) of the Bank of England Act).

In the autumn of 1957 Cobbold, the Governor, started consulting members of the Court somewhat earlier than he normally would do before a change in the Bank Rate. This was because the Chancellor asked him on the Sunday evening for a firm view on behalf of the Bank by the Monday evening. Cobbold therefore had to consult the Committee of Treasury during the Monday, and also wanted to consult other directors whom he thought could best advise him on that particular matter. The purpose of such consultation was not only to secure and formulate the Bank's view, for in making recommendations to the Chancellor about the Bank Rate and other major matters the Governor regards himself as voicing the judgement of the Bank

17

collectively, but to ensure that any specific proposal would be duly observed, for, Cobbold said, it would be 'excessively inconvenient' if a Bank Rate proposal were rejected by the Court.

The economic situation

Throughout the summer of 1957 gold and dollars had been passing out of the country at a dangerously fast rate. At the lowest point of the crisis the reserves had fallen to 1,850 million dollars, which meant that there would have been a total exhaustion within a matter of months (the reserves had not even fallen as low as that as a result of the Suez invasion the previous year). In Professor Lionel Robbins' view, in *Lloyds Bank Review*, 1958, it was clear that if nothing had been done, either devaluation or a repudiation of current obligations was a virtual certainty within a few months.

It is not, therefore, surprising that the Chancellor of the Exchequer was very busy during the summer explaining the Government's policy both to its supporters and to people generally. In addition, in July he gave instructions to the Treasury to consider the possibilities of checking inflation by taking firmer control of money supply in both public and private sectors of the economy.

On Wednesday, July 10th, Mr Peter Thorneycroft (now Lord Thorneycroft), then Chancellor of the Exchequer, opened the new head office of the United Kingdom Provident Institution and said, in his speech, 'It is my intention that the borrowing of money should be as difficult as the real shortage of resources demonstrates to be necessary' (*The Times*, 11 July 1957). His speech on that occasion was regarded by *The Economist* as the first instalment in a campaign to sound, once again, the alarm about inflation

18

(the second was his speech to the National Productivity Advisory Council for Industry on Friday 12th, when he dealt more specifically with costs and prices). *The Economist* said:

> . . . the Chancellor used unexceptionable words and asked the right questions. Do the qualities of thrift and restraint still exist in our Government and in the national character? Has inflation come to stay? Are prices bound to go on rising? Are fixed interest securities a sound investment? (This surely, must be the first time that any British Chancellor has felt bound to pose such a question within the City of London.)
>
> 'How honest,' he asked, 'is our money?' His answer was 'As honest as we choose to make it'. A nation that pays itself seven per cent more for doing no more work (which was his simple shorthand for the rather more complicated economic facts of last year) could not avoid increasing prices against itself. It was for the country to choose. As for the Government's part, it would not hesitate to adjust 'even the most essential investment programme'—though nothing was spelled out in terms, say, of atomic energy, or transport. In any case 'adjustment' is bound to be of programmes, not of current burdens. Credit restriction, he made quite clear, has its part to play in the struggle against inflation; and he pointed to the moderated trend of bank advances in April and May, after the unwelcome increases in February and March.

On July 11th Thorneycroft spent an hour with Conservative back-benchers at a meeting of the 1922 Committeee where he reviewed the economic and financial position of both Britain and the sterling area with special reference to the discussions which took place at the Commonwealth Prime Ministers' Conference. *The Times* reported that 'The Chancellor did not give the impression that the announcement of any drastic new measures to

19

check inflation is imminent. The Government supporters who attended appear to have been anxious rather than critical'.

On July 12th Thorneycroft spoke to the National Productivity Advisory Council for Industry. He said there was no heaven-sent painless and moral solution of the problem of inflation, but in his judgement the Government's policy was a good one: 'It is clearly defined. It is working and will continue to work in the future. We may from time to time adapt or adjust it, but we do not intend to reverse it. . . . We intend to continue these policies.'

On July 13th *The Times* leader writer suggested that if there was not a reasonable response to the Government's call for restraint of demands for increases in wages, 'the Government should convey one other measure to give force to their words. That is that they will be unable to offer any guarantee that the banking system will be permitted to extend additional credit in order to afford full employment for everybody at wage levels substantially higher than those now ruling.'

During the weekend July 13/14th, political speeches showed that some of the Government's own supporters were in a critical and apprehensive mood about the railway freight rates and the inevitable repercussions—there was a particularly well publicised speech by Mr (now Sir) Gerald Nabarro, M.P.

On Monday July 15th, Thorneycroft tried to play down the growing fear of inflation. He explained what he had not meant by his warning words the previous week, that there was after all, no crisis. *The Economist* reported him as saying: 'Exports are rising, production is going up. There is a large volume of investment and a good outlook of a trade surplus with the rest of the world.'

The Ministry of Labour made its regular monthly announcement about the cost of living index on July 15th. The index had risen by one point between May 14th and June 18th. On June 18th the official index figure, which measures changes in the average level of retail prices compared with the level on January 17th 1956 (taken as 100), was 105·7 compared with 140·6 on May 14th.

On July 16th the Cabinet met twice. At both meetings Ministers wrestled with the problem of how the Post Office was to raise an extra £42 million a year to meet soaring costs, without creating a storm of protests in the House of Commons and the country. Mr Ernest Marples, then the Postmaster-General, was present to submit his own proposals and joined in the discussions (though he was not a member of the Cabinet). The morning meeting, at 10 Downing Street, lasted for two hours, but as the Cabinet had not completed its considerations of the proposed new postal charges by lunch-time, they decided to meet again that afternoon in the Prime Minister's room at the House of Commons. The afternoon meeting lasted about an hour and a half, and on July 18th Marples announced increased postal charges in the House of Commons. These included an increase from 2½d to 3d in the basic inland letter rate and an increase from 2d to 2½d in the rate for inland postcards (the 2½d letter rate had operated from 1940).

Criticism among Government supporters continued to grow, and on July 19th, *The Spectator*, a paper not renowned for its criticism of Conservative policies, said :

Mr Thorneycroft has not been able to look complacently over the beginnings of the recovery anticipated in his Budget; instead he has had to issue a series of lugubrious warnings, which can only be interpreted as an admission of failure. . . . By his feeble speeches he has revealed that he is bankrupt of any national economic policy.

21

And if he is not prepared to take the drastic steps that are probably going to be required, there is a real risk that he may bankrupt the country too.

The Statist was similarly critical when, in that week's issue, it commented: 'The Chancellor has made the point that there is no magic formula for stopping inflation. He might have added that, while the Government has employed almost all the known weapons of the disinflationary armoury, it has obviously not wielded them vigorously enough.'

More industrial unrest broke out on July 20th. There was already a strike at Covent Garden over a proposed unified staff system, but on July 20th a strike began of 100,000 busmen employed by private companies. The strike had been called by the unions in support of a demand for an increase in pay of £1 a week.

On July 25th, during the economic debate in the House of Commons, Thorneycroft announced the establishment of 'an independent and impartial council on Prices, Productivity and Incomes'. (This was later popularly known as the 'Three Wise Men', and consisted of Lord Cohen (Chairman), Sir Dennis Robertson and Sir Harold Howitt. It was disbanded in 1962.) He explained that the Council's terms of reference would be 'Having regard to the desirability of full employment and increasing standards of life based on expanding production and the reasonable stability of prices, to keep under review changes in prices, productivity and the level of incomes (including wages, salaries and profits) and to report thereon from time to time'.

At the end of July, Poole, then Chairman of the Conservative Party, was extremely concerned about the inflationary condition of the country, particularly in relation to the political situation, and he 'had conversations on the subject', reporting his concerns to the Prime Minister in August. He felt, as a result of those conversations, that the Prime Minister was also concerned and would take action. But although Poole knew of the sterling problems of India, and other matters of that kind, it was not until the first week in September that he fully appreciated the pressure that was being put on the pound from outside the country. Nevertheless, during the summer, although it was no direct responsibility of his, he gave a considerable amount of thought to what should be done simply because he was so concerned 'about the political repercussions.

Also in July and the earlier part of August, Cobbold, as the Governor of the Bank of England, was contemplating whether a change in the Bank Rate would be appropriate to deal with the economic situation. His main considera-tion at that early stage (July) was the domestic situation (he has since explained that when he came back from his holiday on September 14th the decision on whether the Bank Rate should be changed was dictated more by the foreign situation than the domestic one). He attended the regular Thursday morning meetings of the Bank's Court of Directors on August 7th, 14th and 21st, then he left England for a holiday abroad on August 24th. At each of those three meetings he proposed that there should be no change in the Bank Rate, but he told the Court that he and the Deputy Governor were watching the monetary situation closely. During that period Cobbold was in touch with Sir Roger Makins (now Lord Sherfield) then Joint Per-manent Secretary to the Treasury, and they discussed further disinflationary measures. During their discussions, Cobbold intimated that a rise in the Bank Rate would need consideration in the early autumn. These intimations by

23

Cobbold are the earliest specific mention of considering raising the Bank Rate.

In August the economic situation in Britain continued to deteriorate, and it was aggravated by developments on the Continent.

On August 7th, the Chancellor, before he went on holiday, gave instructions to Makins that during his absence abroad a study should be made in the Treasury of the possibility of bringing about a measure of deflation in the economy. As a result of those instructions Makins spoke to the Governor of the Bank of England, at the Treasury, on August 8th, and he told the Governor of 'the way the Chancellor's mind was working'. A further meeting to discuss the same subject, took place between the Governor and Makins at the Bank of England on August 12th.

Meanwhile, the French government took action to strengthen the franc and there were rumours of a revaluation of the deutschmark. The French Bank Rate was raised from 4 per cent to 5 per cent on August 12th, its highest rate since 1937, and this was accompanied by other measures which were regarded collectively, by *The Economist* as 'almost amounting to a devaluation'. On August 15th the Netherlands Bank decided to raise its discount rate by $\frac{3}{4}$ per cent, from $4\frac{1}{4}$ to 5 per cent. This was an extremely high rate for the Netherlands as the rate had been raised from $3\frac{3}{4}$ per cent to $4\frac{1}{4}$ per cent in the autumn of 1956 (then a new peak for the post-war period). During the April-May period there were also announcements of higher Bank Rates from Switzerland, India and Japan. In July there were announcements of higher rates from Sweden, Belgium and Spain.

These measures led to a wave of speculative selling against sterling, and there were considerable losses from our gold and dollar reserves. The loss from the gold and dollar reserves during August was 225 million dollars, and in September the loss was 292 millions (the August figure was published on September 5th, but the September figure was not precisely known until early October).

On August 19th the Treasury firmly denied rumours which had been circulating on the Continent, that there was an impending devaluation of the pound. On August 20th *The Times* commented : 'Yesterday's strong denial in London was not only an expression of the determination of the authorities to defend the pound at the current rate of exchange : it also implied that they were prepared to do this even at the cost of some loss to the gold and dollar reserves.'

On August 20th *The Economist* analysed the economic situation and advised 'the British authorities' to 'be prepared to take stiff internal measures'. It also commented that 'while few people expect a rise in Bank Rate, nothing is clearer than that there will be no fall'.

On August 22nd the Governor and Deputy Governor of the Bank of England called on Makins at the Treasury. They discussed the studies which the Treasury had made in accordance with the Chancellor's instructions, and the Governor gave his view that a rise in the Bank Rate would need consideration in the early autumn.

Four days later, on August 26th, Makins was present at a meeting of Treasury officials with the Chancellor when there was a discussion on some of the proposed measures to bring about deflation.

On August 27th the Prime Minister summoned the Cabinet to 10, Downing Street. This was their first meeting since Parliament had adjourned for the summer recess on August 2nd. They met for two and a quarter hours in the morning and resumed their meeting in the afternoon. It was believed that Thorneycroft reported to his col-

25

leagues on the talks about inflation which he had been having with members of the National Productivity Advisory Council for Industry.

On August 28th, at a meeting of the Bank of England's Committee of Treasury, Mr (now Sir) Humphrey Mynors, then the Deputy Governor, told the Committee (the Governor was away on holiday) that 'Bank Rate had not come under discussion with the Treasury' but that he was 'keeping it under review', and the next morning he repeated this statement at the meeting of the Court of Directors.

This information given by Mynors is rather curious. The facts are that on August 7th the Chancellor issued his instructions that a study should be made of the possibility of bringing about 'a measure of deflation in the economy'. As a consequence, the next day, August 8th, Makins discussed it with the Governor of the Bank of England. They had further talks on August 12th, and again on the 22nd, and at the meeting on the 22nd the Governor has said that he intimated his view that a rise in the Bank Rate would need consideration in the early autumn. It was after these discussions had taken place that, on August 28th and 29th, the Deputy Governor told the Bank's Committee of Treasury and Court of Directors that the Bank Rate had not come under discussion with the Treasury.

This is curious because it may have one of three possible meanings. The first is that at their meetings on 8th, 12th and 22nd the Governor and Makins did not very seriously discuss the question of a change in the Bank Rate (the Governor just gave his intimation in passing), or, if they did, it was not considered a reasonable course of action and was therefore dismissed without proper discussion. If this was the case, it reflects badly on the Treasury because if they were considering deflationary measures, a

26

change in the Bank Rate should have been one of their main considerations—indeed, many people in the City and some journalists were at that time urging an increase in the Bank Rate.

The second possibility is that the Bank Rate was fully discussed between the Governor and the Treasury and considered as a possibility, but that the Deputy Governor was not fully aware of the discussions, although he accompanied the Governor to the Treasury. If this was the case it reflects badly on the relations between the Governor and his Deputy. For the Governor knew at that time that he would shortly be going on holiday, and it was his responsibility to ensure that his Deputy (who has the full authority of the Governor in his absence) was fully aware of all that had been happening.

The third possibility is that there was a discussion between the Governor and Makins on the possible rise in the Bank Rate, the Deputy Governor was aware of this, but for some reason decided not to tell the Committee of Treasury or the Court that it had happened. If this was the case, it is a poor reflection on the Deputy Governor unless, of course, there is some unknown good reason for withholding such information from those people who were in positions of considerable responsibility.

On August 28th, Mr C. A. S. Cooper, the Investment Secretary of the Royal Exchange Assurance Co, broke his holiday in order to attend the Committee of Treasury meeting of the Royal Exchange Assurance. At that meeting Lord Kindersley, the Governor of the Company, who had just returned from Canada said: 'I have got a most depressing view of the European, particularly the United Kingdom, scene. . . . My counsel to you all is to remain as liquid as possible as an investment recommendation.' From this time Cooper considered that there was a very

27

grave decline in Britain's financial affairs. Although he resumed his holiday after the meeting, he kept himself informed on financial matters through the press.

Mr Harold Macmillan, then the Prime Minister, returned from a short holiday in Scotland on September 6th and held a Cabinet meeting in the afternoon. There were two more Cabinet meetings on September 10th (they lasted a total of four and a quarter hours), and on September 12th there was another Cabinet meeting. Macmillan had previously arranged to leave London again on September 14th to spend another week's holiday in Scotland, but he had to cancel that holiday because of pressure of work. This was a particularly busy time for the Cabinet because, in addition to the serious economic situation, there were developments in the Middle East (President Eisenhower regarded Syria as near to a state of Soviet domination and had arranged for a first consignment of anti-tank weapons and other arms to be delivered by air to Amman in case Jordan should be attacked by Syria), proposed changes in the Government, and the legislative programme for the next session of Parliament to be discussed.

Thorneycroft knew that on September 20th he was due to go to the Washington meeting of the International Monetary Fund. It was clear to him that in order to safeguard the position of sterling and stop the drain on the reserves it was necessary to reiterate and emphasise, before he left for Washington, the Government's intention to hold the exchange rate of the pound at 2·80 dollars. It appeared equally necessary that some statement of his should be backed up by a declaration of policy demonstrating the intention to deal with the inflationary situation at home. For he felt that it was necessary not merely to state the Government's intention, but to say how the Government was going to put its intention into practice.

During September, therefore, the Chancellor was working on these policies with his colleagues and advisers, and he also found it necessary in the first few days of September to consult with certain persons outside government circles (such as the Chairman and Deputy Chairman of London Clearing Bankers), persons whose co-operation was, in Thorneycroft's view, essential for the implementation of his proposals to restrict credit. He also sought confidential advice from two economists—Professors Richard Sayers and Lionel Robbins (now Lord Robbins).

3

Leading up to the decision

'The Bank and the Treasury are in fact separate
institutions arriving at a common policy by
discussion.'
(Thorneycroft, Evidence to the Radcliffe Committee)

September 1st to September 15th

On September 2nd Lord Kindersley, a Director of the Bank
of England and of several other companies, called on
Mynors, the Deputy Governor of the Bank of England, to
discuss the economic situation. From July 11th to August
24th, he had been travelling in the United States and
Canada, and he had returned to England three days earlier
than he had intended because he was disturbed by the
attitude of businessmen in Canada towards the pound
sterling. He was shocked by what was going on in Britain
and thought something had to be done.

Kindersley and Mynors discussed, among other things,
the pressure on the pound and the possibility of raising
the Bank Rate, but not in relation to a particular date,
and Kindersley told Mynors about his visit to North
America. He said he was really shocked at what was going
on in Britain and that something had to be done. He said
that, in his opinion, 'Bank Rate had got to be raised, and
raised properly, but that it was no good doing it unless
the Government were going to make a statement as well,
so that it would be really worthwhile, and that everybody

in this country was going to be made to realise what the situation was and pull their own oar'.

After seeing Mynors, Kindersley thought 'it was quite inevitable' that the Bank of England's course would coincide with the course he thought ought to be pursued. But he also thought that the other things the Government were going to do, what the Government would say, and in particular what they would say about spending and how they would face up to wage claims in the nationalised industries, were more important than the Bank Rate.

On the same day that Kindersley first saw Mynors, September 2nd, the Chancellor of the Exchequer sought confidential advice from Sayers and Robbins. Sayers had served in the Ministry of Supply and the Cabinet Office from 1940 to 1947 and was (in 1957) a member of the Radcliffe Committee on the Working of the Monetary System and holder of the Sir Ernest Cassel Chair of Economics at the London School of Economics, and Robbins had been Director of the Economic Section of the Cabinet Office during the war years and was (in 1957) Professor of Economics at the London School of Economics. The Chancellor discussed monetary policy with each of them.

It is, of course, expected that in such a matter as this the Chancellor of the Exchequer would seek advice from eminent economic advisers, but that he should seek advice from Sayers and Robbins is particularly interesting for three reasons.

First, in order to get advice from Robbins, Thorneycroft had to telephone to Switzerland, where Robbins was on holiday, and ask him to come back to London. According to Samuel Brittan there were two reasons for this. The Chancellor knew and respected Robbins and wanted to make sure that Robbins thought his proposed measures were sensible. He also wanted him to speak to Macmillan (though there is no published record that he actually did), 'who was far from keen on Thorneycroft's proposed measures', and, in any case, Brittan adds, Robbins 'is an extremely impressive person to have on one's side' (Brittan, 1964, 191).

Secondly, from 1947 to 1961 the Economic adviser to Her Majesty's Government was Sir Robert Hall, but there is no record that Hall was consulted on these matters. One would have thought that whilst the Government was entirely free to seek advice from whoever they chose, they would also seek advice from their Economic Adviser. And if he *was* consulted it is rather curious that, although he was a confidential adviser, his name was never mentioned at the Inquiry.

Thirdly, it is interesting that the Chancellor was in a position where he felt such a particular need for outside advice. Some interesting light is thrown on this by Samuel Brittan, who must have interviewed Thorneycroft on this topic.

In the first place, 'Thorneycroft was disturbed by the thought that he, as a lay Minister, knew more about finance than Sir Roger Makins, his Permanent Secretary' (*ibid*, 186) (this was very different from his experience at the Board of Trade, where he worked very happily with Sir Frank Lee, with whom he had a close sympathy).

In the second place,

> The Treasury itself presented a confused and divided picture during this period, and the official Treasury advice which Mr Thorneycroft received from the Permanent Secretary, Sir Roger Makins, was opposed to what he did . . . Mr Thorneycroft felt that his only consistent supporter near the top of the hierarchy was Sir Leslie Rowan who was in charge of external finance. Thorney-

croft formed the impression that Sir Roger Makins was against what he was doing, but he had no alternative advice to offer except to ride out the storm. There may have been a case for doing nothing, but it would have to be argued with great clarity, force, and ruthless facing of possible consequences if it was to convince a Chancellor who had just seen a quarter of his gold reserves disappear within a couple of months (*ibid*, 190-191).

Thorneycroft worked out the main lines of policy with the help of his two ministerial colleagues at the Treasury, Mr Enoch Powell, the Financial Secretary, and Mr Nigel Birch, the Economic Secretary (who exercised a dominating influence extremely unusual for a junior Treasury Minister). 'It was they who were largely responsible for turning the anti-inflationary policies into a crusade. Needless to say, the Bank of England sounded the alarm in the summer of 1957 and backed the Treasury Ministers all along the line' (*loc. cit.*).

In the third place, Thorneycroft was worried because not only was his Department not supporting him, the Cabinet also was not supporting him, and in particular, the Prime Minister was not keen on his proposals (*loc. cit.*). Macmillan's views on the economy were always coloured by his acquaintance with unemployment in Stockton-on-Tees in the inter-war period—he always feared that prosperity and full employment could be too easily sacrificed by a one-sided devotion to 'sound money' at the expense of other objectives (*ibid*, 180).

On September 3rd, the day after he had seen Kindersley, Mynors wrote letters in his own hand (a very unusual procedure) to Mr M. J. Babington Smith, Mr W. J. Keswick and Sir Alfred Roberts. He wrote to them because they were three of his colleagues who were out of London and he did not expect to see them back for the best part of

33

a fortnight. In each personal letter Mynors told them substantially what he had told the Court on the previous Thursday. He referred to the August exchange figures because he did not want them to be ignorant of the general worsening financial situation which he had been reporting to the Court of Directors, and explained that discussions were proceeding about the measures that might be taken to deal with the situation. He added that the measures to deal with the situation that were under discussion might eventually include action on the Bank Rate, but that the matter was quite open and undecided. He said that the letter should not, however, be taken as a warning that they might be asked to return to London early, and finally, he asked them to destroy the letter.

W. J. Keswick received the Deputy Governor's letter the next day, whilst he was on holiday in Scotland, and this placed him in a very difficult position. Among his other directorships he was on the board of Jardine, Matheson and Co, and therefore had a responsibility to advise them. But at the same time he had a duty not to disclose anything directly or indirectly in relation to the Bank Rate, and he was then officially learning for the first time that a change in the Bank Rate was under consideration. In addition, the unusual manuscript nature of the letter from Mynors would probably have enhanced its significance. After he had read the letter he destroyed it as requested.

The problem with regard to Jardine, Matheson, was, briefly, that Mr H. M. D. Barton, the company's agent in Hong Kong, had been eager for about a year to sell some of the firm's gilt edged stock. W. J. Keswick had not been encouraging him but it was immediately obvious to Keswick when he had received the Deputy Governor's letter that any decision made in Hong Kong would now be even more important to the firm.

34

Meanwhile, on the same day, September 4th, Mynors attended the meeting of the Bank of England's Committee of Treasury, but he barely mentioned the exchange situation beyond saying that it was substantially unchanged from the previous week, and that the discussions about the measures to deal with the exchange situation, which he had then referred to, were continuing.

In the afternoon Mynors saw the Chancellor of the Exchequer and discussed with him the question of bank advances. The Chancellor agreed that Mynors should speak to Mr D. J. Robarts, the Chairman of the Committee of London Clearing Bankers. They just mentioned the possibility of a change in the Bank Rate, but they agreed that the subject did not arise at that stage. After this, Mynors spent the rest of the afternoon meeting various people to discuss bank advances.

On the same day the Chancellor had a conversation about the economic situation in broad terms with Sir Oliver (now Lord) Franks, who was Chairman of Lloyds Bank Ltd, and Deputy Chairman of the Committee of London Clearing Bankers.

On September 5th, at Mynors' request, Robarts, as Chairman of the Committee of London Clearing Bankers, and Franks, his deputy, called on the Deputy Governor. He told them that the exchange situation was giving the Government cause for anxiety and that the Chancellor of the Exchequer was considering a further restriction of bank advances. A discussion followed, but no mention was made of the level of interest rates or any proposal for a change in that level.

The next day, Makins, who had been on leave from August 29th to September 5th, had lunch at the Bank of England and had a general talk with the Deputy Governor. The talk covered, among other things, the proposed measures including a possible increase in the Bank Rate.

At 11.15 a.m. on September 9th, Robarts, accompanied by Franks, again called on the Deputy Governor at the Bank of England. And at 11.45 all three went to see the Chancellor of the Exchequer, who was accompanied by Makins, at the Treasury. This meeting was again concerned with measures to restrict bank advances (it was not until September 19th that Robarts learned of the decision to raise the Bank Rate).

Thorneycroft told them that he required a limitation of bank advances and explained his reasons for the request. He told them that he was also contemplating parallel action in the public sector, that was to say, he intended to restrict the level of public investment to £1,500 million a year for the next two years. The Chancellor explained that he wanted to make it absolutely plain at home and abroad, before he went to the meeting in Washington of the International Monetary Fund, that the Government intended to hold the exchange rate of the pound at 2·80 dollars, and that positive steps were being taken to implement that intention.

At that meeting Franks remarked that higher interest rates for advances made by banks might help in restricting such advances, but there was no discussion or further reference to the matter. Robarts made some reference to the fact that an increase in the price of money might assist the measures of which the Chancellor was speaking, but the point was not taken up. There was no reference at all to the Bank Rate.

During the week following September 9th, Thorneycroft had a further preliminary discussion with the Deputy Governor of the Bank of England about the possibility of raising the Bank Rate. But although they recognised that the Bank Rate might have a part to play in the deflationary measures they were considering, they thought it better to defer any definite discussion until after the Governor himself had returned on the 15th or 16th.

At the meeting of the Bank of England's Committee of Treasury on Wednesday morning, September 11th, the Deputy Governor told the Committee in general terms of the discussions in which he had participated with the Chancellor and his officials and with the representatives of the clearing bankers. He also told them that the programme was still quite undecided, but that, depending on how it went, they might have to consider whether there was a part to be played by a change in the Bank Rate. A discussion followed on the possibility and propriety of raising the Bank Rate in the circumstances then existing.

On the same day the Chancellor again saw Mynors and the Chairman of the Committee of London Clearing Bankers. Thorneycroft once more outlined the problem to them, explaining the strain on the reserves and his intention to hold the exchange rate of the pound at 2·80 dollars. He also told them that he was going to make a statement before he left for Washington, and that the statement would affect the control of the money supply, the restriction of bank advances and restriction on investment in the public sector. But no reference was made to interest rates or to the Bank Rate.

Also on Wednesday 11th, the Chairmen of the eleven leading Clearing Banks were summoned by the Chancellor and he told them to tighten the squeeze on overdrafts.

At the usual weekly meeting of the Court of the Bank of England on Thursday September 12th, the Deputy Governor told the Court substantially the same as he had told the Committee of Treasury the previous day, though perhaps in somewhat less detail. He said that in his view

37

a sharp increase in the Bank Rate might be necessary as part of the combined operation, but there was no specific reference to the date on which that combined operation would have to be effected.

Later in the day Mynors saw Sir Charles Hambro, Kindersley and Sir Alfred Roberts. They had all been at the Court meeting, but they once more, briefly, mentioned the economic situation and the possibility of raising the Bank Rate.

On September 12th there was a further meeting between the Chancellor, the Deputy Governor and the representatives of the London Clearing Bankers; Makins was also present. They discussed the restriction on bank advances but did not mention the Bank Rate. There was, of course, further discussion on succeeding days, among senior officials inside the Treasury, about the possibility of a rise in the Bank Rate.

The Deputy Governor also called on Makins at the Treasury and they discussed the contents of a draft of a statement to be made by the Chancellor the following week, about the proposed measures. There was no reference in the draft to the Bank Rate. Mynors said that he would be prepared to discuss the question of raising the Bank Rate with the Chancellor on the following day, but that any recommendation to the Court would have to await the return of the Governor. When asked at the Inquiry, Mynors agreed that there was therefore a possibility that the Chancellor's statement might have to be made on Tuesday, September 17th. They also discussed the timing of the announcement of any change in the Bank Rate and related matters.

On September 13th Mynors again saw the Chancellor of the Exchequer and they had a short discussion about the Bank Rate. Although no figure was actually mentioned it was accepted that it was with a view to increasing the Bank Rate.

Meanwhile, Sir Edmund Compton, then Third Secretary at the Treasury, prepared a statement dealing with the consequences of the rise, or possible rise, in the Bank Rate at different levels. And the Chancellor of the Exchequer and Mr Harold Wilson had a talk at Wilson's request.

Wilson told Thorneycroft that Mr Hugh Gaitskell, then the Leader of the Labour Party, was proposing to refer in a speech at the American Chamber of Commerce, to the economic situation, and that Gaitskell was anxious to be reassured of the Government's intention to maintain the parity of sterling. Thorneycroft gave that assurance, and also said that he was proposing to make a statement to that effect before leaving for Washington.

On September 14th Cobbold returned from his holiday and immediately went to see the Deputy Governor at Mynors' house in the country, where they spent the next twenty-four hours together. Mynors brought the Governor up to date with the developments during the three weeks of Cobbold's holiday, including the discussions the Deputy Governor had had in the previous few days, discussions which included the possibility of a change in the Bank Rate.

On the morning of the next day, Sunday September 15th, Cobbold and Mynors were joined in the country by Mr (now Sir) Maurice Parsons, an executive director of the Bank of England, for a talk on the overseas and exchange aspects of the financial situation.

In the afternoon Cobbold and Mynors returned to London and at 5.30 p.m. had a short formal discussion with Makins. At 6.00 p.m. they all went to 11, Downing Street for a meeting with Thorneycroft, Birch and Makins. At the 6.00 o'clock meeting Cobbold said that he had not

39

been able to discuss the question of the Bank Rate with his colleagues, other than the Deputy Governor and Parsons, but he added that his provisional view was in favour of an increase and that the increase should be to seven per cent.

The Governor was asked to let the Chancellor have the Bank's firm view about the nature and timing of the Bank Rate change by the following evening, and this he promised to do. He also undertook to discuss with the representatives of the clearing banks the reference to bank advances to be made in the statement which the Chancellor was proposing to make.

Cobbold left with the impression that the Chancellor was already in consultation with his ministerial colleagues. Makins had made notes of the whole discussion at Number 11, and later circulated the notes to the Chancellor and senior Treasury officials.

4

How the decision was made

Mr Cross: When would you say that effectively the deci-
    sion to raise the Bank Rate was taken, if I can put it
    in that way?
Mr Cobbold: Effectively, I would say, on the Wednesday
    morning about lunch time after I had been informed
    that the Government would approve and after I had
    put the matter to the Committee of Treasury and they
    had approved the submission to the Court of Direc-
    tors.
Mr Cross: I suppose theoretically the final decision is only
    taken when the Court makes its decision on the Thurs-
    day?
Mr Cobbold: Oh, certainly.

(Bank Rate Tribunal Evidence)

Monday September 16th

Monday September 16th was the first day of concentrated
activity. One has the impression that so many people had
returned from holiday that work was able to proceed.

For example, Mr C. A. G. Cooper, the Investment Secretary of the Royal Exchange Assurance, returned from holiday to his office at 10 a.m. Whilst on holiday he had been
keeping himself informed through the press, but he was
very depressed because he felt that the Government's
handling of the situation was inadequate and that the
country was moving swiftly towards a currency crisis. He
therefore talked to stockbrokers and generally made in-

41

quiries about the spirit in the City, to see whether others were as apprehensive about the situation. He gained the impression that the Government Broker was 'grooming' the gilt-edged market for a new Government Refunding Issue. Among other measures, Cooper thought that the Bank Rate ought to have been raised to six per cent a month earlier.

At 11.15 a.m. Cobbold, who, it will be remembered, had also just returned from holiday, saw Robarts, the Chairman of the Committee of London Clearing Bankers, and at the Governor's request they discussed that part of the Chancellor's draft statement which related to bank advances. But they did not mention the Bank Rate. A re-draft of the statement was later sent to Robarts and about midday or in the early afternoon Robarts telephoned his agreement to the draft.

In accordance with the undertaking he had given on the previous day, at the meeting with the Chancellor, Cobbold next consulted members of the Court of Directors. He was accompanied by the Deputy Governor and he saw Lord Bicester, Mr (now Sir) Geoffrey Eley, Sir Charles Hambro, Mr Basil (now Lord) Sanderson, and Mr M. J. Babington Smith at 12 o'clock, and Kindersley at 12.45 p.m. He told them about the state of the exchanges and gave details of his discussions with the Chancellor about the measures to protect sterling. He also told them that he proposed, subject to the Chancellor's approval, that those measures should include a two per cent rise in the Bank Rate on September 19th. However, this was hardly surprising news for any of them in view of the strain on sterling and the fact that the week before, at the Committee of Treasury, discussion had taken place on the possibility of raising the Bank Rate.

Cobbold also explained to the Tribunal that it was the normal procedure for the Governor to consult members of the Court before there was a formal recommendation to it for a change in the Bank Rate, but there were really two reasons for the consultations at that particular time. The main object was to be able to present the Chancellor, that evening, with the Bank's firm view, and this meant that his consultations took place rather earlier than usual. The secondary object in obtaining the views of those people at that stage was to be sure of their support when the proposal came before the Committee of Treasury and the Court of Directors. This was, for example, why Cobbold told Kindersley of the proposed rise at that particular stage. The Governor wanted to feel that, on a question as important as that, he had his Court with him. He would be able to discuss the rise in the Bank Rate with his Treasury Committee on Wednesday, the day before the rise, but he would not have been able to discuss it with the other members of the Court until Thursday. He had to think of the awkwardness of the position, after he had made all his arrangements, if at the meeting of the Court on Thursday someone like Kindersley, who was a Director, but not on the Committee of Treasury, stood up and said: 'I just do not agree with it'.

This form of consultation between the Governor and members of the Court is quite normal practice, but on this particular occasion Cobbold thought he started making detailed consultations a day or just a shade (sic) earlier because of his undertaking to the Chancellor to give him a firm view on the Monday evening. Normally he would not need to be quite so clear and definite until he was making a proposal to the Committee of Treasury on Wednesday morning.

The 12.45 p.m. meeting with the Governor was the first time Kindersley heard of the proposal to raise the Bank Rate by two per cent, and he gave his agreement right

43

away. The Governor also mentioned that he was having discussions with the Government about other measures to accompany the Bank Rate change.

Kindersley went to Lazard Bros, for lunch, and afterwards attended the Executive Committee meeting of the British Match Corporation. Then, at approximately 5 o'clock (Kindersley told the Tribunal he thought he saw the Governor at about 4.30, but when told that Cobbold had said it was 5 o'clock he agreed to that time because 'he would know better than I'), Kindersley saw the Governor again and told him that on further consideration he was very much concerned about the effect which an immediate rise in the Bank Rate might have on the underwriting of the Vickers' issue of £30 million of securities. He said that, in his opinion, if the Vickers' issue was underwritten on the Wednesday and the Bank Rate was raised on the Thursday, the whole of the City would wonder whether the Bank had really been justified in allowing the Vickers' issue to be made, because obviously the underwriters would be left with a very large amount of their underwriting, and there would be definite indigestion in the underwriting market in the City for weeks, if not months, to come. Kindersley said he was worried about the effect of this on the Bank's public relations.

Cobbold thought that Kindersley had a very proper and relevant point and he discussed the question with the Deputy Governor and the Chief Cashier. (It was the Chief Cashier who had arranged the timing of the issue, because, Cobbold explained to the Tribunal, it was 'an operational matter, not a policy one'. However, the fact that the timing was so inopportune raises the question of why the Chief Cashier had allowed it. As the Chief Cashier has since become Governor it seems that the Bank did not regard his decision as a serious error of judgement. One

44

wonders whether the operational decision was a further example of poor communications or of poor general management at the Bank.) Cobbold also asked the Deputy Governor to telephone Bicester and ask him whether anything could be done about it. Having done this, Cobbold concluded 'very definitely' that there was nothing to be done. But Kindersley continued to feel worried and therefore saw the Governor about it again the next day.

At one o'clock W. J. Keswick, a Director of the Bank of England and of a number of other companies, went, as he often did, for lunch at the Bank of England. It was quite a casual visit, he went without warning. And as it was his first day back at work after his holiday he looked into the Deputy Governor's room for a few minutes before lunch, just to say he was back.

This was the first time Mynors had seen W. J. Keswick since he wrote the letter to him on September 3rd, so Mynors let him know that the discussions he had mentioned in his letter were still going on. He added that if the Government's programme, when it was finalised, seemed to indicate that a very sharp rise in interest rates would be useful they would have to consider doing it (this was what he had been saying at the previous meeting of the Court). But their discussion was otherwise in fairly general terms and covered the August exchange figures, the German elections and the approaching I.M.F. meetings. The Deputy Governor gave Keswick the impression that there was a general realisation that the world was expecting the deutschmark to rise and the pound to fall in value. Keswick left the Bank at about 2.30 p.m., but did not return to his office that day.

At 6 p.m. Cobbold called on the Chancellor, who had with him Makins and Rowan, the Second Secretary at the

Treasury. Cobbold explained that although he had not yet been able to speak with all his colleagues, he was able to give the Chancellor a firm view about the Bank Rate. The Bank, he said, considered that the proposed increase to seven per cent on September 19th was desirable. The Chancellor then asked for the arguments in writing to support that view, and Cobbold presented the arguments, as requested, the next morning.

Cobbold told the Tribunal that he thought the *effective decision* to raise the Bank Rate was taken on the Wednesday morning about lunch time, after he had been informed on the telephone by Makins that the Government would approve the decision, and after he had put the matter to the Committee of Treasury and they had approved the submission to the Court of Directors. But *theoretically* the decision was taken only when the Court made its final decision on the Thursday. This still left it up to the Governor to make a different proposal to the Court, if there was some violent change, but in the absence of a violent change, the effective decision was taken on the Wednesday.

After the 6 p.m. meeting between Cobbold and Thorneycroft, Cobbold had a further discussion with Makins and Rowan about the paragraph in the Chancellor's draft statement dealing with the restriction of bank advances.

Sometime during the day, E. W. Maude, Principal Private Secretary to the Chancellor of the Exchequer, heard that the Bank Rate might go up to seven per cent. He told the Tribunal that he probably heard it from the Chancellor himself. It is somewhat surprising that a man in a position so close to the Chancellor, who sees all the papers of any importance that pass through the Chancellor's office, should become aware of this so late, and it rather suggests that the Treasury had not considered it very seriously as part of the deflationary measures they had been considering in accordance with the Chancellor's instructions in August.

Tuesday September 17th

By September 17th rumours were beginning to circulate. For example, Mr Sidney Gampbell, the Financial Editor of Reuters, heard a rumour that there was an impending directive from the Treasury to the banks, that would, in effect, put a rigid ceiling on bank advances. He therefore telephoned Mr C. Raphael, a Treasury Press Officer, to inquire about it, but Raphael said there would be no directive.

However, the information services within the civil service were beginning to organise themselves for an announcement. Mr J. McIntosh, who had ten years experience as a Civil Service Information Officer, and who was at that time Principal Information Officer at the Ministry of Labour and National Service, was told that there would be an important announcement from the Treasury on Thursday. He was told to stand by for Wednesday afternoon when he and the Chief Information Officer were to be briefed by the Minister.

At 10 a.m. Mr (now Sir) Richard Fraser, the Joint Director of the Conservative Research Department, went to the Treasury to meet the Chancellor as arranged at Fraser's request the previous week, but when he arrived he saw E. W. Maude, who told him that the Chancellor could not see him as arranged, but hoped to see him before he went abroad.

At 11.30 a.m. Cobbold spoke to Sir George Bolton and Sir John Hanbury-Williams. The discussion with them followed the same lines as that which Cobbold had had the

47

previous day with Bicester, Eley and others. Therefore, by 11.30 the Governor had seen eight of the sixteen Directors of the Bank.

At 12.30 p.m. Makins telephoned Cobbold about the part of the Chancellor's draft statement relating to the restriction of bank advances, and Cobbold asked for an opportunity to bring Robarts to see the Chancellor. This was arranged, and at 2.15 p.m. Cobbold, accompanied by Robarts, called on the Chancellor at 11, Downing Street. The Chancellor was accompanied by Makins and E. W. Maude, and they spent just under half an hour together in further discussion on the draft, but without mentioning interest rates. After Robarts had left, Cobbold had a short talk with the Chancellor about the Bank Rate and confirmed the Bank's view that there should be a two per cent rise.

Sometime during the day there was a meeting in the Treasury between Thorneycroft, Birch, Makins and other Treasury officials, at which they discussed the proposal to raise the Bank Rate by two per cent.

At 3 p.m. there was a Cabinet meeting, which considered the terms of Thorneycroft's announcement about the economic measures which the Government was intending to take other than the change in the Bank Rate.

The Cabinet approved Thorneycroft's suggestion that in order to get the maximum possible support for his policy some advance guidance should be given to the Press and also some advance warning to those most immediately affected. Lord Mills (Minister of Power) and Mr Ian Macleod (Minister of Labour) were to share this work with Thorneycroft and they each planned that the next day they would see some of the people involved.

The reason for the consultations was that Thorneycroft considered it essential, in view of the growing pressure on the pound, that he should get as quickly as possible the maximum support for the policy he was putting forward. He explained to the Tribunal that he was concerned that there should be a willingness to give the policy a chance to work, not only at home, but also that it should be fully presented overseas. For he felt that unless people both inside and outside the country understood the nature of the operation he was directing, there might be comment in the Press which could have imperilled the whole operation and made his task in Washington very difficult indeed. He considered that if he failed with this operation to stem the drain on sterling it was unlikely he would have another chance.

As far as Thorneycroft could see, the world was interested in whether Britain was prepared to take the necessary decisions to deal with inflation. He therefore felt he had to describe a series of measures that were very controversial, and were potentially very unpopular, and see that they were put over at the same time as he knew in his own mind that the rise in the Bank Rate was going to be announced. He told the Tribunal that his object was to win the confidence of the Press and get a good Press, and he added that it was not an uncommon thing to see journalists for this purpose. For example, Sir Stafford Cripps did the same thing in 1948, before publishing the White Paper on Wages, Profits and Prices.

In the course of the Cabinet's discussion the question was raised whether those measures would be sufficient by themselves to meet the economic situation, or whether they should be reinforced by an increase in the Bank Rate to either six per cent or seven per cent, and it was pointed out that, by tradition, variation of the Bank Rate was not a matter for decision by the Cabinet. It was agreed that the point should be left for further discussion by the Prime

49

Minister with the Chancellor of the Exchequer and the Governor of the Bank of England.

Later in the afternoon the Chancellor asked Cobbold to call on him at 9 p.m. that evening for a talk with the Prime Minister.

Meanwhile, early the same afternoon, Kindersley discussed privately with Bolton, another Director of the Bank of England (whom both the Governor and Kindersley regarded as being one of the greatest foreign exchange experts in the world), the repercussions on the City of a possible rise in the Bank Rate on the day after the Vickers' issue had been underwritten. Bolton agreed that the problem was important and advised Kindersley to go and see the Governor again. So Kindersley went straight away, at 3.30 p.m., to see Cobbold and repeat, even more forcibly, his fears about the effect of a rise in the Bank Rate on the Vickers' underwriting arrangements, and about possible repercussions on relations between the City and the Bank. Kindersley asked whether it was possible to postpone the increase in the Bank Rate until the Chancellor of the Exchequer had gone to the meeting of the International Monetary Fund, but the Governor replied that 'practically every Cabinet Minister . . . would be in Canada or America' and so it could not be done then.

Having been convinced that it was not possible to postpone the Bank Rate rise (though it is difficult to understand why Kindersley was convinced by this argument as a Bank Rate decision is not one for the Cabinet, and on this occasion only two members of the Cabinet, the Chancellor and the Prime Minister, were involved), Kindersley asked the Governor for permission to examine with Bicester the possibility of postponing the Vickers' issue. Kindersley had known for days, as a result of what he has called the 'preliminary feelers' which the underwriting businesses put out in the City, that the issue was going to be under-written. Kindersley assured the Governor that he would see Bicester (who already knew of the proposal to raise the Bank Rate) alone. The Governor then gave his permission and on the same day Kindersley telephoned Bicester, who agreed to call at Kindersley's office at about 4.30 p.m., on his way back from another meeting in the City.

Cobbold already knew, because he had considered the matter himself the previous day, that absolutely nothing could at that stage be done about the Vickers' issue. In fact, as he explained to the Tribunal, he was not at all concerned about Kindersley's motive for seeing Bicester. His reason for consenting to their meeting was quite simple, he wanted to make sure he had Kindersley's support for the Bank Rate change.

When Kindersley saw Bicester he explained his reasons for asking if the issue could be postponed, but Bicester told him that he had signed the contract with Vickers at about 2.45 p.m. the previous day and offers of sub-underwriting had been posted to various sub-underwriters that evening.

Kindersley said that in view of what they both knew was probably going to happen, he was fearful that the issue would be entirely left with the sub-underwriters, and he wondered if there was any way in which the issue could be postponed. Bicester did not think this could be done because Morgan, Grenfell and Co were already committed to Vickers, and a large majority of the sub-underwriters had accepted the offer of sub-underwriting. Therefore the only people who could possibly postpone the issue would be the directors of Vickers, and that would be an impossible decision for the directors to take without consulting the shareholders, as the company was now sure of the money. As a result, Bicester felt there

51

was nothing could be done about it, and Kindersley agreed.

When asked by the Attorney General at the Inquiry why it had not been left to the Governor to see Bicester, Kindersley pointed out that it was perfectly natural for one Director of the Bank of England to go and talk to another colleague at the Bank about the Vickers business. Also Morgan's (Bicester's firm), and Lazards (Kindersley's firm), were probably closer than any other two issuing houses and they 'discuss intimate details of every kind and description'. Kindersley did not think Bicester would find it in the least surprising that Kindersley should go to him and say, 'Look here, Rufie, is it too late to stop this business or not?' Bicester knew that Kindersley had talked to the Governor and Kindersley felt entitled to say to Bicester, 'I have discussed this with Jim—with the Governor—and I am coming on to see you'.

Mr Oliver Poole, a director of several companies, and at that time also Chairman of the Conservative Party Organisation, who had gone to Stoke-on-Trent on business on September 16th, returned to London by train on 17th. As soon as he was back in London he went straight to the Conservative Central Office and arrived at about 4.30 p.m. A message was waiting for him that the Prime Minister wanted to see him. Poole arrived at 10, Downing Street, between 6 and 6.30, and at about 7 p.m. he saw the Prime Minister, who had with him Lord Hailsham (now Mr Quintin Hogg) and Mr Edward Heath, then the Government Chief Whip. The Prime Minister told Poole that the Chancellor was going to make a statement on Thursday and he therefore wished the announcement of the change between Hailsham and Poole (Hailsham was to be appointed Chairman of the Party and Poole to become Deputy Chairman) to take place on Wednesday and not on Thursday as had provisionally been arranged between Poole and Heath.

Poole said that could be arranged. The Prime Minister gave him the impression that he considered the Chancellor's statement very important, and that he wished the general publicity that would be given to it to receive considerable attention. No reference was made to the Bank Rate, and Poole left 10, Downing Street, at about 7.30 p.m.

Shortly after 9 p.m. Cobbold called on the Chancellor at 11, Downing Street, as arranged that afternoon. The Chancellor was accompanied by Makins, Compton and E. W. Maude. They discussed the whole monetary question, including the Bank Rate proposal, and Cobbold recommended an increase in the Bank Rate to seven per cent. Cobbold also told the Chancellor that Robarts, the Chairman of the Committee of London Clearing Bankers (he is also Chairman of the National Provincial Bank and holds a number of other directorships), was very anxious to see him that evening, in order to discuss again the terms of that part of the Chancellor's draft statement that referred to the limitation on bank advances.

Then, at 10 p.m. the Chancellor went on with Cobbold to see the Prime Minister next door. Makins and Compton went with them, and Mr F. A. Bishop, then the Prime Minister's Private Secretary, was also present at the meeting. The Governor repeated his recommendation that the Bank Rate should be raised to seven per cent, but no firm decision was reached. The Prime Minister said he wanted more time before making up his mind whether the Government should agree to the Bank Rate being raised, and, if so, to what figure.

While the Chancellor was with the Prime Minister, E. W. Maude, who had remained at number 11, telephoned

53

Robarts at his home, and at about 11 p.m. when the Chancellor had returned, he telephoned him again and asked him to call at 11, Downing Street. Robarts arrived shortly afterwards, though he told the Tribunal he was with the Chancellor and Governor at about 10.30 p.m. (as Maude was leaving to go home he saw Robarts in the Chancellor's drawing room). The Chancellor and Robarts resumed the discussion they had been having earlier in the day. Robarts felt it was part of his function as Chairman of the Clearing Bankers to consider the effect upon banking of the proposed credit restrictions, and that his opinion about the effects would be important to the Chancellor and others considering the restrictions. At the meeting, besides the Chancellor, Robarts and Cobbold, there were Makins and Compton. One or two verbal alterations were made in the statement about bank advances and then Robarts said that the draft would be acceptable to his committee. Robarts also made the observation that in his view a higher level of interest rates would be a material help to the request the Chancellor was making for tighter money and a more intensified credit squeeze. Nothing was said in reply to that observation. Cobbold showed the Chancellor and Makins a draft he had prepared for an informal press release. Robarts repeated his observation about interest rates to Cobbold as they left the meeting, but Cobbold made no reply.

Wednesday September 18th

At 10 o'clock the next morning, Wednesday September 18th, Thorneycroft saw the Prime Minister and they reached the conclusion that a Bank Rate increase to seven per cent would be justified. At 11 a.m. the Chancellor went to the Treasury and told E. W. Maude, his Principal Private

Secretary, that the Prime Minister and he had agreed that it would be right to increase the Bank Rate to seven per cent. Maude then saw Makins and it was agreed that Makins should inform Cobbold. Makins therefore telephoned Cobbold at 11.45 a.m. and told him that the Government would accept a decision by the Bank on the lines discussed the previous evening. The rest of Makins' morning was spent with the Chancellor, discussing various aspects of the proposed measures and the handling of the statement.

It is rather curious that the Prime Minister and the Chancellor reached their conclusion at 10 o'clock but that the Governor of the Bank, who was responsible for the decision, was not informed of this conclusion for another hour and three-quarters—in fact, only three-quarters of an hour before he was to attend the meeting of the Bank's Committee of Treasury. It is also interesting to note that it was actually Makins who telephoned the Governor to tell him 'that the Government would approve a decision by the Bank on the lines discussed on the previous evening'. (This was a curiously guarded way of expressing the decision when Makins had 'a direct line' to the Governor. Either that direct line is not secure, or one is left wondering what other reason there could be for such a guarded expression on a secure telephone, or why Makins told the Tribunal he used that particular expression.)

Shortly after 10 a.m. Cobbold, who was driving himself along the Embankment to the City, met Kindersley who was travelling in the next car, and as he wanted to know whether Kindersley was still worried about the Vickers' issue, he asked Kindersley to change cars and accompany him. Kindersley changed cars and explained the result of his talk with Bicester the previous afternoon. He also confirmed that although the Vickers' issue could not be postponed he would support the recommendation for a rise in the Bank Rate.

At 12.30 Cobbold presided at a meeting of the Bank of England's Committee of Treasury. Those present were Mynors (the Deputy Governor) Hanbury-Williams, Sanderson, Bolton, Eley, Bicester, Hambro, and Babington Smith (the last two were specially invited, the others were all regular members of the Committee). The Governor recommended to the Committee for submission to the Court the next day, that the Bank Rate be increased from five per cent to seven per cent, and the Committee approved the recommendation.

During the morning Lord Moore (now the Earl of Drogheda), Managing Director of the *Financial Times*, attended a Board meeting of the St Clement's Press, and whilst he was there he received a telephone message that the Chancellor wished to see him on a private matter at 3 p.m. As he and Thorneycroft were personal friends, he assumed the meeting would be concerning some personal matter. But when Moore called and saw the Chancellor, alone, at 3 o'clock, he learned that the Chancellor had a statement on financial policy which he was going to make the next day. Because Moore was not concerned with the editorial comments he suggested that it would, perhaps, have been more appropriate if the Chancellor had seen his editor. Thorneycroft said that he had already considered doing that, but had, in the end, invited Moore. He also said that in the statement he would be announcing measures to strengthen the external and internal value of the pound, and the chief purpose of his measures would be to control the supply of money. As far as capital expenditure by nationalised industries and government departments was concerned, he was going to lay it down that for the next two years, expenditure in terms of pounds should be kept to the level of the current year. And in the case of private expenditure, he was going to tell the banks that he wished advances to be kept to the same level during the next twelve months as they had been during the current twelve months, and therefore, any increase in advances to one customer would have to be compensated by a decrease in advances to another customer. In their discussion there was no reference to the Bank Rate.

After leaving Downing Street Moore returned to his office, where he saw Mr (now Sir) L. G. Newton, the Editor of the *Financial Times*, and Mr Wincott, the Editor of the *Investor's Chronicle*. While Wincott was with Moore they rang the Treasury to inquire whether Wincott could see anyone at the Treasury the next morning, because the *Investor's Chronicle* would then be going to press and he would have liked to be in a position to publish something in the paper so that it appeared to be up to date with its comment. This was arranged, and Wincott went to the Treasury at about 12.15 p.m. the next day.

Early in the afternoon Mynors again called on Makins at the Treasury, and Makins gave him the final draft of the concluding paragraph of the Chancellor's statement (the paragraph on the rise in the Bank Rate), which had been prepared at a meeting in Makins' office that morning. Mynors accepted it, subject to confirmation by the Governor. Makins and Mynors also discussed and agreed the line which the Bank should take in dealing with the Press about the rise in the Bank Rate. Later in the afternoon Mynors confirmed the Bank's agreement with the Chancellor's statement, and Makins subsequently informed the Chancellor and the other officials concerned. He also sent a copy of the draft final paragraph to E. W. Maude, who showed it to the Chancellor, and it was then sent across to the Prime Minister's Private Secretary.

Later in the afternoon Maude heard on the telephone, 'in sufficiently guarded terms' that the Prime Minister had agreed to the draft. (Again, one wonders why secure telephones are not used at the Treasury or if they are used why the Chancellor's Principal Private Secretary was not using one. If he was in fact using such a telephone it is even more curious why he should tell the Tribunal he heard of the Prime Minister's agreement 'in sufficiently guarded terms'.) The draft that had been sent to the Prime Minister was not returned. Maude kept the original, and either that night or the next morning he stapled it to one of the duplicated copies and gave it to a typist for the final version. There were several copies of the draft, one went to the Chancellor, one to the Economic Secretary, and six or seven to senior Treasury officials, all the spare copies were placed in a cupboard in Maude's room.

Maude explained to the Tribunal that it was in the afternoon, after the draft of the concluding paragraph of the Chancellor's statement had been settled, that the Chancellor decided he would see certain representatives of the press in a series of personal interviews, to explain the significance and purpose of the economic measures. He seemed to remember this quite clearly and explained that he did not personally make the arrangements for the meetings, but he asked Mr Downey, a colleague in the Chancellor's office to do the telephoning. Mr S. C. Leslie, Head of the Information Division at the Treasury, also helped with organising the interviews.

It is strange that this was so clearly Maude's recollection of what had happened, as Thorneycroft told the Tribunal he saw the representatives of the press as a result of a decision at the Cabinet meeting on September 17th (it met at 3 p.m.), and Macleod explained that he saw the representatives of the T.U.C. and Employers as a result of a decision of 'a policy committee of the Cabinet'. It seems most likely that Maude was mistaken (the memories of busy people can be unreliable), as Moore received his invitation in the morning—although according to Maude it was clearly in the afternoon that he asked Downey to do the telephoning to the newspaper representatives. It is a pity that the Tribunal did not clear up this confusion— for they also must have been confused (or were not, following the evidence very closely) as they heard the evidence from Moore and Maude on consecutive days at the beginning of the Inquiry, and they did not hear the evidence about the Cabinet meeting until towards the end of the Inquiry, nearly three weeks later. To anyone examining the evidence day by day, this may at first suggest that someone other than Downey had telephoned the message to Moore. It was in any case peculiar that Moore, rather than the Editor of the *Financial Times* should have been invited. But Mr Donald Tyerman, the Editor of *The Economist*, gave evidence that he, too, received a message in the morning inviting him to see the Chancellor in the afternoon. The simplest explanation is, therefore, that it was just Maude who was mistaken. However, this does not satisfy every aspect of the anomaly because one would think that if it had just been a mistake on the part of Maude, the evidence of everyone else would be in agreement. The fact remains, that whilst Moore and Tyerman received their invitations in the morning, the other press representatives received their invitations quite late in the afternoon (e.g. Mr S. Gampbell, of Reuters, said he was telephoned by Leslie at about 4.40 p.m. and Mr D. Mc-Lachlan, of the *Daily Telegraph*, also told the Tribunal that he was telephoned 'in the afternoon').

Birch, the Economic Secretary to the Treasury, saw the Chancellor several times during the day, and spent the

59

first part of the afternoon with him. At one of their morning meetings the Chancellor told him that the final decision to increase the Bank Rate to seven per cent had been taken as far as he and the Prime Minister were concerned, and that they would give their consent if the Governor of the Bank of England saw fit to do it. Mr Christopher Bennett, Private Secretary to the Economic Secretary, told the Tribunal that he first heard of the political decision, subject to the Bank's decision, about lunchtime. Bennett probably heard of the decision by seeing a draft of the Chancellor's statement complete with its 'ninth paragraph'. Of course, this also meant that Bennett's personal assistant, Mrs Cameron, would be another person who knew of the decision by the afternoon, because she would be concerned with enveloping copies of the statement for transit under 'Top Secret' cover.

At 3 p.m. the Chancellor saw Moore of the *Financial Times* and at 3.30 he saw Sir William Haley, Editor of *The Times*. In the early part of the afternoon, certainly when he saw Moore, the Chancellor was alone, but at the interview with the Conservative representatives he was accompanied by Birch. The Chancellor explained that certain measures were going to be taken, and he thought it essential that exactly why they were being taken should be made clear to these people beforehand. The Chancellor said the Government was going to clamp down on the supply of money, he referred to cuts in capital investment levels and said they were going to be held up for two years in the public sector and one year in the private sector. Haley, who had previously been Director-General of the B.B.C., thought from his experience that the Chancellor's policy would not work unless something was done about interest rates. Haley told the Tribunal that he was not thinking of the Bank Rate but of something more long term, and he expressed his opinion to the Chancellor, but the Chancellor said he could not discuss those things then. The interview lasted only about ten minutes.

Meanwhile, at 3.30 p.m. Poole attended a press conference with Hailsham at the Conservative Central Office, but at 4 o'clock he left to see the Chancellor at the Treasury in response to a telephone message he had received from the Treasury earlier in the day. He was very anxious that his departure from the press conference should not be taken as a discourtesy to Hailsham, as his sole reason for being there was to show that he and Hailsham were going to work together. As he left he excused himself by saying that he was leaving for a meeting at the Treasury.

Poole, Fraser (the Joint Director of the Conservative Research Department), and Mr David Dear, the Head of the Economic Section of the Conservative Research Department, arrived at the Treasury between 4.10 and 4.15. On arrival they went straight to the Chancellor's office. The meeting with the Chancellor began a little late, and Birch went in with them. The Chancellor explained to the Tribunal that he saw them, with the knowledge and approval of the Prime Minister, because he appreciated that the moment his policy was announced, Poole and the Conservative Central Office would be faced with many inquiries and he thought Poole should be equipped to answer them. He told them precisely what he had told the press, and nothing was said at the interview about raising the Bank Rate. Fraser thought that as there had been credit squeezes before, the public reaction might be not to see anything very new or dramatic in the measures, and that therefore the public reaction might not be sufficient. He expressed his view at the meeting but there was no discussion about it. The meeting lasted about half an hour, and was therefore considerably longer than some of the

61

interviews with press representatives; Haley for example, was with the Chancellor for only about ten minutes.

At the end of the meeting someone, probably Poole, asked that a summary of the information might be given. Maude was not present at the meeting, but Poole, on his way out, told Maude that the Chancellor had said he could give him a piece of paper summarising the items in the verbal statement they had just heard. Maude made a slightly non-committal reply about seeing what he could do, then Poole and Fraser walked with Birch to his office to wait for the document. Dear followed them a few moments later.

Maude cut off very neatly with a pair of scissors, the bottom two inches or so of a copy of the draft of the Chancellor's statement that contained the words '9. (Paragraph to be added)', and handed the draft to Bennett, the Economic Secretary's Private Secretary, to give to Poole when he left the Economic Secretary's room. Maude then went back to his own office, and at the beginning of the next meeting, when he was sitting next to the Chancellor, the Chancellor said that no document bearing any relation to the Bank Rate should be given to Poole. Maude said that he had anticipated his wish, and assured him that it was all right.

When the document was handed to Poole he glanced at the top sheet and noticed that it was headed 'Top Secret', but he did not notice whether all the pages were of the same length. Poole passed the document to Dear and then returned to the Conservative Central Office. Dear took the statement, which amounted to an advance hand-out of the statement to be issued to the press the next day, home to study.

Before Poole left the Central Office at about 6 p.m., he spoke to Mr Sims, the Chief Publicity Officer. Poole told him that the Chancellor was going to make an important announcement the next day before leaving for the International Monetary Fund meeting, that they attached considerable importance to publicity, and that therefore Sims was to make sure he received from the Chancellor of the Duchy of Lancaster the same briefing as the press. Finally, he indicated that the announcement would be, in general, of a restrictionist nature.

The next person to see the Chancellor was Tyerman, Editor of *The Economist*. During the morning Tyerman had received a message inviting him to see the Chancellor at the Treasury, and he saw the Chancellor shortly after 4.30 p.m. The Chancellor told him he thought it would be convenient for him to know about the statement that he was going to issue the next day. It would say two things. First, that he proposed to announce a ceiling in money terms upon the public investment programmes; and secondly, a ceiling upon bank advances. The Chancellor explained that this was necessary in order to assert a control upon the supply of money, and he also pointed out that these measures were necessary because monetary measures themselves were not enough. Although nothing was said about the Bank Rate, Tyerman was left with the very strong impression that the measures the Chancellor proposed to announce on the following day were instead of a change in interest rate policy. And Tyerman felt that this was a 'Hamlet without the Prince of Denmark'. He was not long with the Chancellor, and was back in his office shortly after 5 o'clock. After Tyerman had left, the Chancellor saw Mr Paul Bareau, City Editor of the *News Chronicle*, at 5 p.m. and told him substantially the same as he had told Tyerman and the others, and there was no mention of the Bank Rate.

When Bareau left Thorneycroft he was accompanied

63

from the Chancellor's room to the exit of the Treasury by Leslie, the Head of the Information Division of the Treasury (it was, incidentally, Leslie who had telephoned Bareau to invite him to see the Chancellor). On the way, Bareau, recognising that it was Wednesday, asked Leslie if it would not be justifiable to raise the Bank Rate in the present circumstances. Leslie threw Bareau off the scent by answering with a question. He said, 'Given all the other measures we are taking, do you really think there is the slightest significance in Bank Rate?' Bareau told the Tribunal that when he left the Treasury at about 5.20 he gave the Bank Rate no further thought because he had received the impression that it was not going to be changed.

At 5.30 Thorneycroft saw McLachlan, the Deputy Editor of the *Daily Telegraph*. McLachlan had been contemplating writing a leading article discussing the international monetary factors which were affecting the weakness of the pound. When they met, the Chancellor said that he had come to the conclusion that monetary measures were not enough to defend the pound, and he went on to describe the measures he intended to take without mentioning the Bank Rate. The Chancellor also mentioned that he was going to make a statement to lobby correspondents at 12 noon the next day. The subject of the Bank Rate did not occur to McLachlan. On his way out, he talked to Leslie as they went along the corridor to the exit, and for three or four minutes they discussed the political impact of the measures that had been discussed, but they did not mention the Bank Rate.

The last journalist to be seen by Thorneycroft on the 16th was Gampbell, the Financial Editor of Reuters. Leslie had telephoned Gampbell at 4.40, because he had shown some personal interest in measures that might be taken, and Leslie said that the Chancellor would be ready to see him if he liked to call at the Treasury at 6.30. At 6.30 Thorneycroft outlined to Gampbell all the measures he would be announcing the next day, except the Bank Rate. At 9 p.m. Leslie telephoned Gampbell at home, primarily to give him some idea of the length of the next day's state-ment because it was important for Reuters to know as soon as possible whether it merited sending it textually in the overseas news. Leslie had a general chat and gave Gampbell his idea of the sort of cable the Embassies might be receiving. But the Bank Rate was not mentioned.

At 8.45 p.m. McLachlan telephoned E. W. Maude, to let him know that he was proposing to publish a statement in the next day's *Daily Telegraph*, which, though written by Mr F. Whitmore, the City Editor, before McLachlan had seen the Chancellor, nevertheless contained a specu-lative reference to matters which the Chancellor had that afternoon disclosed to him in confidence. Maude thanked him for telephoning.

At 10.15 p.m. Newton, Editor of the *Financial Times*, learned that there had been a statement in the first issue of the *Daily Telegraph* (for 19th). He told his political correspondent to make contacts in official circles to see what he could do about it. Within a quarter of an hour the political correspondent was able to tell Newton that the Private Secretary to the Chancellor knew about the *Daily Telegraph*'s statement.

Thus Thorneycroft saw on Wednesday afternoon some of the people whom it had been agreed by the Cabinet should be given some warning of the measures about to be taken. Others whom it was felt should be told were seen by Mills and Macleod.

At 11.45 a.m. Mills, then Minister of Power, saw Lord Citrine, then Chairman of the Central Electricity Author-ity, to explain the economic measures, apart from any reference to the Bank Rate, that were to be announced the next day, in so far as they affected the electricity industry. Mills gave the information from a prepared brief (similar to the one the Chancellor was using) and the next day, when the announcements were made public, he sent a copy of the brief to each of the chairmen he interviewed. At each of the meetings, except those with Sir Christopher Hinton and Sir Henry Self, Mills was accompanied by Sir John Maud (now Lord Redcliffe-Maud), then the Permanent Secretary to the Ministry of Power. Mills and Citrine were together until 12 o'clock, when Mills and Sir John Maud went to the inaugural meeting of the Electricity Council.

At about one o'clock, just before lunch, Mills spoke privately to Hinton, Chairman of the Central Electricity Generating Board, and Self, Chairman of the Electricity Council, and gave them the same information as he had given to Citrine.

After lunch, soon after half past two, he returned to the Ministry of Power and about an hour later saw, for the same purpose, Sir Henry Jones, Deputy Chairman of the Gas Council.

During the afternoon Macleod, then Minister of Labour and National Service, also as a result of the decision of the policy committee of the Cabinet, saw representatives of the Trades Union Congress and British Employers' Confederation; Sir Harold Emmerson, then Permanent Secretary at the Ministry of Labour, was present at both meetings.

At 5.45 p.m. Macleod saw Sir Vincent Tewson (who had received a telephone message the previous day inviting him to see the Minister), Sir Tom Williamson, and Mr T. Yates together, and told them of the pending developments. A short discussion followed, during which Williamson expressed the desire that the Government should be

66

selective in their cuts of the investment programme in the public sector, and suggested that building controls, among other things, might be reimposed. Nothing was said about the Bank Rate and the meeting ended about 6.30.

Macleod then saw Sir Colin Anderson and Mr Pollock, representing the British Employers' Confederation, and gave them information similar to that he had given to the representatives of the T.U.C. The representatives of the Confederation said they would discuss the impact of the measures with their Council and they told Macleod they would call a meeting the next morning to discuss what to say to the Press after the Chancellor's statement had been made. According to Macleod, those representatives left him shortly after 7 p.m., but Pollock told the Tribunal they were with Macleod for only 10-15 minutes.

At some stage it was planned that Macleod should see Mr Richardson, his Public Relations Officer, and his deputy, to prepare them in case there were questions from the press, but Macleod cancelled the meeting because he felt there was nothing he could tell them that could not wait until the next morning.

At 2.10 p.m. Cobbold saw Mr Lawrence Cadbury and at 2.40 he saw Sir Alfred Roberts. They were both Directors of the Bank of England and Cobbold gave them the same information about his proposal on the Bank Rate as he had earlier given at the meeting of the Committee of Treasury.

Between 3 and 3.30 p.m. Mr G. D. Kirwan, Secretary and Controller of the National Debt Office, paid his customary weekly visit to the Bank, where he met Mr (now Sir) Leslie O'Brien, then the Chief Cashier. They first talked about the origin of the money that was coming into the funds he was concerned with, then O'Brien said, 'We are going to do something tomorrow.'

By this, Kirwan understood that the Bank Rate would be moved, and this meant that he was expected to refrain from asking the Chief Cashier to do any deals in stock, which was the normal thing they would discuss in the latter part of their talk. It was normal for Kirwan to be given an intimation before a change in the Bank Rate, then he would do no dealings until after the announcement was made. He was not told how much the rate would be moved, or which way, but he agreed with the Tribunal that it was easy for him to guess which way.

Between 3.30 and 4 p.m. Mr W. J. H. de W. Mullens (now Sir William Mullens), the Government Broker, made his usual daily report to the Chief Cashier of the Bank of England. The principal purpose of this daily report is to explain to the Chief Cashier what had happened in the market during the day. On this day, Mullens said the market closed steady, though short dated securities were dull. O'Brien told him that the Bank Rate was going to be raised from five per cent to seven per cent the next day. This meant that he would not deal on behalf of the Bank the next day until after the Bank Rate announcement. (Consequently there was no free market on the Thursday until after the Bank Rate announcement was made. But this was not unusual as the Government Broker never deals on official account on Thursday mornings before the announcement of the Bank Rate, whether or not there is to be a change.)

At about 4.30 p.m. W. J. Keswick was summoned to the Bank of England by the Deputy Governor and told for the first time that the next day the Court of Directors would be asked to approve a recommendation that the Bank Rate should be increased to seven per cent. Keswick immediately disclosed to the Deputy Governor that his company had that day received a large selling order of gilt-edged from Jardine, Matheson and its associated companies in Hong Kong. The Deputy Governor advised him that he should not attempt to cancel the sales.

Thursday, September 19th

Thorneycroft's first engagement on Bank Rate day was at 9.45 a.m. when he saw Mr R. H. Fry, the Financial Editor of the *Manchester Guardian*, at 11, Downing Street (the appointment had been made by telephone the previous afternoon). The Chancellor explained to Fry the measures, apart from the rise in the Bank Rate, that he was intending to take to deal with the situation, as he had told the other press representatives the previous day. Fry felt that the Chancellor was hoping for his support and co-operation.

After seeing Fry, the Chancellor saw Sir Norman Kipping, the Director of the Federation of British Industries.

At the same time, 9.45 a.m., Fraser of the Conservative Research Department, and Sims, the Chief Publicity Officer of the Conservative Party, attended a meeting with Dr Charles Hill (now Lord Hill), then the Chancellor of the Duchy of Lancaster. The course of their discussion was on similar lines to the discussions at the Treasury the day before, but in less detail. They also discussed the cuttings from that morning's *Daily Telegraph* and *Financial Times*, which Sims had seen, but which Fraser had not seen at that stage. Arising from the *Daily Telegraph* cutting, Sims asked if there was any likelihood of a change in the Bank Rate. Hill replied non-committally, with words to the effect that 'That is always possible'.

Simultaneously, at 9.45, Mills was seeing Sir James Bowman, Chairman of the National Coal Board, and he told him what he had told Lord Citrine and the others the previous day.

69

At 10.30 a.m. at the Treasury, the final draft of the Chancellor's statement left E. W. Maude's possession and went for copying. Then began what Maude called the 'considerable last minute rush' to get the five or six hundred copies prepared in time for the deadline of 11.45, as it was anticipated that the Bank of England would make their announcement at about 11.50 and that would be immediately followed by the release of the Chancellor's statement.

The Cabinet met at 10.30 and continued sitting until approximately lunch time. They were informed that the Prime Minister had reached the conclusion that the Government should accept the view of the Bank of England that the Bank Rate should be increased to seven per cent, and the Cabinet took note of that conclusion. This was the first time that most of the Cabinet Ministers knew that a definite decision to raise the Bank Rate had been made, although they had known since the 17th that an increase was being contemplated.

Also at 10.30, at the Bank of England, Cobbold saw Sir Harry Pilkington (now Lord Pilkington), another Director of the Bank, and informed him of his proposal that the Bank Rate should be raised from five per cent to seven per cent.

Later, at 11.45, Cobbold presided at the meeting of the Court of Directors and presented the proposal of the Committee of Treasury that the Bank Rate be raised by two per cent. The Court approved the proposal.

5

The Bank of England and the Treasury

'I remember . . . how the monetary situation
appeared to us at the Treasury—at least at the
ministerial level. It appeared like an antiquated
pumping machine, creaking and groaning, leaking
wildly at all the main valves, but still desperately
attempting to keep down the level of water in the
mine.'

(Thorneycroft, 1960, 1)

The Bank and the Treasury are coming closer together.
Just how close they have become is revealed in this study
of the decision to raise the Bank Rate in September 1957.

It was the Bank that had the final responsibility for
decisions to change the Bank Rate, although the Treasury
has power, under the Bank of England Act, 1946, to issue
directions. The interesting thing is that as far as we know,
directions have never been issued. The Bank has always
made its decision in the light of what it knew would be
acceptable to the Chancellor. In a sense it was not therefore the pure decision of the Bank, but the decision of
what the Bank felt ought to be done, when it had considered the very important factor of what the Chancellor
would accept. Cobbold explained to the Tribunal, 'In the
event of a proposed change it is the normal practice for the
Governors to ascertain whether the Chancellor would agree
before they make the proposal to the Committee of Treasury on the Wednesday morning.' Keswick, in his evidence

71

before the Tribunal, said he thought a rise in the Bank Rate depended entirely on the politicians at that time. Kindersley was told by the Governor that the timing of a Bank Rate change was affected by the availability of Cabinet Ministers when the decision was announced.

This is an interesting development in the relations between the Bank and the Treasury. Earlier in this century the Bank had a considerable amount of freedom in these matters. After the passing of the Bank of England Act the development from that position was partly recognised. Changes in the Bank Rate were still to be the Bank's decision, but it was openly said that such decisions were not made without the agreement of the Chancellor of the Exchequer. How this was arranged is seen in this case study.

At the Bank Rate Tribunal Cobbold argued that the Bank of England is not a mere operating department under the Treasury. The suggestion that it was, had been stimulated by quoting Sir Stafford Cripps who, on one occasion at a press conference referred to the Bank of England as 'my creature'. But that was not, as has been popularly attributed, the end of Cripps' statement for he added, 'but like many creatures, it sometimes goes its own way' (Bareau, 1964, 41). One certainly has the feeling that, in 1957, the Bank had very little opportunity to go its own way in the decision to raise the Bank Rate.

Development of the relationship

In the nineteenth century the Bank was virtually independent of Government control. The Prime Minister, Lord Liverpool, speaking in the House of Lords in 1822, described as extraordinary and injurious the refusal of the Bank of England to discount at a lower rate than five per

72

cent, when the market rate of interest was not more than four. 'Finding it impossible,' he said, 'to induce the Bank to lower the rate of interest on their accounts, conformably with expectations held out in 1819, His Majesty's Government resolved on borrowing four million pounds on Exchequer Bills from the Bank with a view to applying that sum in some manner to the relief of the country' (Hawtrey, 1938, 14).

Shortly before the First World War the Bank of England stated officially that 'the Government has no voice in the management of the Bank' (Dodwell, 1934, 75), but during the War, Bonar Law, then Chancellor of the Exchequer, regarded the Bank of England as the wartime servant of the Government, and the policy it pursued in financial affairs had to conform to the will of the Treasury. In 1917, there were disagreements between Treasury officials (Sir Robert Chalmers and J. M. Keynes) and the Governor of the Bank of England (Lord Cunliffe), which led to the Governor writing to Lloyd George, the Prime Minister, '. . . I cannot remain a mere figurehead acting under men in whom I have no faith. . . .' As a result, Bonar Law seriously contemplated transferring the Government's account to one of the Joint Stock Banks. But in November 1917 the Directors of the Bank of England nominated Sir Brian Cockayne as Governor in place of Lord Cunliffe and there was no further trouble between the Bank and the Treasury while Bonar Law remained Chancellor of the Exchequer (Blake, 1955, ch. 22). Lord Beaverbrook later observed: 'The authority of the Treasury has been explicitly asserted over the Bank of England. That authority was never relinquished. Bonar Law had established a principle on which the final seal was fixed when in 1946 the Socialist Government nationalised the Bank of England (Beaverbrook, 1956, 108).

Lord Norman (Governor 1920-1944) was impressed by Mr Wm. Middleton Campbell (Governor 1907-1909), 'he always said that Campbell was "a man"; in putting up Bank Rate on his own responsibility without waiting for the Court "he was dead right"' (Clay, 1957, 56). But in 1926, in evidence to the Royal Commission on India Currency and Finance, he explained the relations between the Bank and the Government in this way: 'I look upon the Bank as having the unique right to offer advice and to press such advice even to the point of nagging; but always of course subject to the supreme authority of the government.' And in 1937, explaining the relations of the Bank and the Treasury on the management of exchange policy to the Governors of the Empire Central Banks, meeting in London, Norman said: 'I am proud that I am a Central Banker talking to Central Bankers; but I would ask you to remember that I am the instrument of the Treasury. The two are, of course, not incompatible, especially in these days, and I would not say that I am in any way embarrassed by divided loyalties' (Clay, 1957, 437). It was also a saying of Lord Norman's when Governor that 'my job is to think out what the government wants before it knows it'.

Sir Ernest Musgrave Harvey, then Deputy Governor of the Bank of England, gave the following explanation to the Committee on Finance and Industry, 1931 (the Macmillan Committee):

> We, on our part, never venture to interfere on any question that can be considered a political question, unless we are asked to express an opinion as to what the financial effect of a certain political operation may be. If we are asked, we give our advice, but we never seek to interfere in politics. The Treasury, on the other hand, are good enough to reciprocate; that is to say, that,

whilst we keep them fully informed as to the general trend of affairs in the City as to any occurrences of importance affecting the position of finance and credit, they do not seek to dictate any alternative line of financial policy if we, in our judgement, consider a particular line of policy essential for the protection of the country's main reserves.

In the House of Commons Debate on the Bank of England Bill in 1945, Gaitskell, though he acknowledged that the Government had effectively controlled the Bank during the war, and that in the eight or so years before the war control had increased, pointed out that the Bank had not always been so co-operative. He mentioned two cases as recent as 1939 when the Bank had exercised an independent influence. The first was on the occasion of the Czech gold episode, and the second was on the raising of the Bank Rate in that year. He said:

> I do not think that any hon. Member would maintain that before 1932 it was the regular custom to consult the Treasury, even on the matter of Bank Rate. It has certainly always been my impression that when the Bank Rate went up in 1929 to six per cent the Government were not consulted at all; but there is a very recent case. At the outbreak of war in 1939 the Bank Rate was put up to four per cent. There may be, again, hon. Members present who recall the circumstances of the time. There was some indignation. After a bit of agitation, in about two months, I think, the Bank Rate, which went up in August, was brought down in October to three per cent. I do not know whether the Bank of England at that time consulted the Chancellor of the Exchequer. Either they did, in which case the Chancellor of the Exchequer at the time was singularly ill-advised to agree, or, as I suspect, they did not.

In 1959 the Radcliffe Committee on the Working of the Monetary System considered that the 'function of the central bank is clearly seen to be that of acting as a highly skilled executant in the monetary field of the current economic policy of the central Government,' so that

> the problem of finding the proper relationship between the two resolves itself into the one of making sure that the exchanges between the two bodies are organised in such a way that the Bank contributes to the Government's discussions on policy the advice and suggestions which its unique operational experience and contacts qualify it to offer, while the Government on its side is careful to associate the Bank with the formulation of those decisions on economic policy in which monetary operations are capable of taking a part.

However, the Committee has also explained that 'It would be unrealistic . . . to regard the meeting of the Court as the source of effective decisions on policy made by the Bank' and 'the Committee of Treasury can be treated without qualification as the voice of the Court. . . . It (the Court) treats the Committee of Treasury as its "conscience in these matters".'

Whilst the Bank of England is one of the principal authorities concerned with the framing and operation of monetary policy, 'it follows that this policy, whatever form it may take from time to time, must include the general planning of monetary policy and monetary operations and that the policies to be pursued by the central bank must be from first to last in harmony with those avowed and defended by Ministers of the Crown responsible to Parliament'. The Committee did not share the view that 'the public interest requires that the central bank should be assured complete independence from political influence', but on the other hand, they did not 'advocate the view that the Bank's position should be regarded as that of a rather exceptional Government department. . . . The true position . . . is that the Bank carries an equal measure of responsibility, to advise to the best of its ability, and, having advised, to execute within the limits of the determined policy'.

In a paragraph primarily concerned with the Bank Rate, the Committee said:

The present system involves continuous and confidential exchanges between the Bank and the Treasury. . . . But just because they are, and must be, to a large extent confidential they tend to obscure the reality of the division of responsibility between the parties. The fixing of Bank Rate has presented itself to us as an instance of this. In form a Bank Rate change appears as a decision of the Court; in practice, by an understanding which long precedes 1946, no change of Bank Rate is announced without the prior approval of the Chancellor of the Exchequer. In form a change in Bank Rate is proposed to the Chancellor by the Governor on behalf of the Bank; in fact all decisions about the level of Bank Rate, whether to move it or not to move it, are decisions of significant importance to the Government's general economic policy, if only for their possible psychological impact. In our view the true responsibility for decision lies today with the Chancellor of the Exchequer, not with the Bank; and it would be better that this could be made explicit by the announcement being made in the name of the Chancellor and on his authority.

In practice, there is a great number of these 'continuous and confidential exchanges between the Bank and the Treasury'. At the top policy level, there is regular contact between the Chancellor and the Permanent Secretary on behalf of the Treasury, and the Governor and Deputy Governor on behalf of the Bank. The senior members of the Treasury visit the Bank regularly, occasionally for lunch as well as for purposes of business and there is a very close relationship between the Head of the Finance group of divisions in the Treasury and the Bank.

77

The Radcliffe Committee was told that in the Bank itself, there is a daily meeting of the Governor, Deputy Governor, executive directors and the Chief Cashier. They hold regular weekly meetings with senior officials and advisers to review both domestic and overseas questions, and more comprehensive monthly meetings to consider statistical and economic reports. There are also frequent *ad hoc* meetings to discuss general or particular matters of policy. These may be called by the Governor, Deputy Governor, or one of the executive directors, and are usually attended by the officers and advisers concerned. For example, when a major aspect of monetary policy is under discussion, the normal 'team' would be the Governor, Deputy Governor, one or more of the executive directors, the Chief Cashier and his deputy, and the advisers who specialise in economic matters. On major questions of overseas policy the 'team' would be the Governor, Deputy Governor, one or more of the executive directors and the heads of the departments and advisers concerned with the particular problem at issue. In order to keep theory and practice as close together as possible, frequent contact is encouraged, and takes place, between heads of departments and advisers; and both heads of departments and advisers always have access to the Governor, Deputy Governor, and executive directors, to enable them to put forward suggestions and comments.

In the overseas field, the Treasury relies heavily on technical assistance and advice from the Bank, and both in Whitehall meetings and in overseas negotiations it has become normal practice for the Treasury to be assisted by Bank officials on technical subjects.

In the field of domestic policy the Treasury and the Bank each have responsibilities. The Bank has the first responsibility for the management of the money market, including the fixing of the Bank Rate and the management of Issue Department securities. Although, by statute, this responsibility lies with the Bank (unless it is given directions by the Treasury), in practice, while accepting this responsibility it has been the policy of the Bank to consult, and in the last resort defer to, the Government.

Indeed, after the rise in the Bank Rate from five per cent to seven per cent on Monday, November 23rd 1964, there were many rumours concerning the relations between the Governor (on behalf of the Bank) and the Chancellor of the Exchequer (on behalf of the Treasury). On November 29th *The Observer* stated that Lord Cromer, then the Governor, had recommended a Bank Rate rise for November 12th and sterling had suffered because it was not raised. Rumours were so widespread that on December 8th, 1964, Sir Stephen McAdden, M.P. tabled a question to the Prime Minister in the House of Commons, about the tenure of office of the Governor of the Bank of England. In a supplementary question he asked whether there had been any recent attempt by the Governor to terminate his tenure of office by premature resignation, but no further information resulted as Mr George Brown, answering for the Prime Minister, said that the supplementary question did not arise from the original question. There is certainly no record of any other occasion when it has even been rumoured that the Governor has recommended a change in the Bank Rate and his recommendation has not been accepted by the Chancellor of the Exchequer. It may be that, after all, the Bank has become a creature of the Chancellor.

The contacts between the Bank and the Treasury are detailed and numerous. For example, in the last three months of 1958 the contacts were counted and the details given in evidence to the Radcliffe Committee. During those three months the Governor and Deputy Governor had over 60 personal discussions with ministers or with officials of the Government. Attendance by executive directors, officials and advisers at meetings in Whitehall numbered over 300; in addition over 400 letters were written by the Bank to Whitehall and some 1,300 telephone conversations took place on policy matters. And these figures do not take account of the large volume of routine communications (amounting to several thousands) on banking, exchange control and statistical matters. Although many of the contacts between the Bank and the Treasury below Governor level are operational contacts, that does not mean that they are insignificant, for, as Sir Edmund Compton, then a Third Secretary at the Treasury, told the Radcliffe Committee, 'a lot of policy consists in the way you carry out operations. You are forming a policy as you operate.'

It is therefore not surprising that Makins, also in evidence before the Radcliffe Committee, described the relationship between the Bank of England and the Treasury as 'an intimate day to day working relationship at the top level and all the way down'.

The development of this relationship between the Bank and the Treasury is more the result of practice and of personal relationships and customs, than it is the result of statutes. It has already been seen how difficult it is to learn details of this relationship. Even in 1957 the role of the Chancellor in Bank Rate changes was not as clear as it is now, mainly as a result of the statement in the House of Commons by Heathcoat Amory on November 26th 1959 (see below p. 86).

Recently, there may have been a further development. On February 25th 1965, Sir Cyril Osborne asked the Chancellor of the Exchequer, in a parliamentary question, if he would reduce the seven per cent Bank Rate. The Chancellor replied 'I will reduce the Bank Rate as soon as I judge the state of the economy will permit. . . .'

The Chancellor's reply contained no recognition at all, even in a purely courtesy fashion, of the responsibility of the Bank in this matter. It is a clear example of the acceptance of authority by the Chancellor over the Bank, and the time may now be appropriate for more public recognition of this development. Perhaps the Governor of the Bank of England should be given the status of a Joint Permanent Secretary to the Treasury and the Bank should become a special sort of government department (a departmental service within the civil service, like the Inland Revenue department). Perhaps, even if the staff of the Bank do not become civil servants, there should be greater opportunities for exchange of staff between the Bank and the Treasury; this was recommended by the Radcliffe Committee, and Thorneycroft has commented that 'an exchange of staff between the Bank and the Treasury is an admirable idea, and an increase in research work in these fields seldom comes amiss . . .' (Thorneycroft, 1960, 13).

The Report of the Radcliffe Committee said that 'The Bank of England stands as the market operator between the public sector (to which it belongs) and the private sector.' It then went on to observe:

in evidence to us, Bank of England witnesses sometimes drew a distinction between on the one hand activities in which the Bank is the agent of the Treasury and on the other hand 'the affairs of the Bank' (using the phrase of the 1946 Act) in which the Bank is supposed to have a wider measure of autonomy or at least a greater responsibility to press its own view . . . We found that during this decade this distinction has had no practical force. . . .

Consequences for decision making

One consequence of this very close relationship is that, as Cobbold explained to the Radcliffe Committee, it is very difficult to say exactly where ideas start from. He said:

> What happens in practice is that I see the Permanent Secretary to the Treasury once or twice a week. Sometimes we agree about everything, sometimes we do not. Sometimes one of us has a suggestion to put forward, sometimes the other has a suggestion. I repeat, the relations (between the Bank and the Government) are very much those of a bank and customer over a wide field. I think I can say that relations have been extremely close. Certainly throughout the period while I have been Deputy Governor and Governor, successive Chancellors have been good enough to take me very closely into their confidence on any matters affecting financial administration. Sometimes they take my advice, sometimes they do not. I have found it very difficult to say just where any particular idea starts or finishes, or exactly where the initiative comes from. . . . [However] in matters like Bank Rate and interest rates and credit policy the initiative normally rests with the Bank of England. There again, week after week, sometimes more often, one is obviously discussing these matters with the Chancellor. I could never say at a precise moment whether an idea originally started with us or with the Treasury. It is very difficult to say, but by and large we should regard the first responsibility about Bank Rate, monetary policy and so on as lying with the Bank.

Similarly, Makins told the Radcliffe Committee, 'I feel some difficulty in trying to describe in detail how a particular decision may be arrived at, because all the elements which go to forming a decision are not in certain cases within officials' knowledge.'

Normally, (invariably in recent practice) a Bank Rate

decision is made by the Court after the Governor has assured himself that the Chancellor would approve the decision. But, according to Cobbold, 'it would be inconceivable' for a Governor to recommend to the Court a change in the Bank Rate which he did not know that the Chancellor would approve, and it would be equally inconceivable for the Court to make a change in the Bank Rate of which they knew the Chancellor would disapprove.

Cobbold explained to the Radcliffe Committee:

If we were to come to a position where agreement was not possible quite a lot of things might happen between that stage and the final stage of deferment. I do not want to put this as if it was something which regularly happens, or which I envisage as likely to happen at all frequently. I can foresee a position where I should have to say: 'I am afraid that the Court would not agree to that,' and the Chancellor would say: 'I am afraid that the Government would not agree to that.' In that event I imagine that one would go back and have another talk. I can envisage circumstances in which the Court might say: 'We are not quite happy about this, but if it is made quite clear that this is the Government's responsibility we will execute on that basis.' That would mean that I would call for directions. If it came to that point (it is a little bit difficult to envisage the exact circumstances) the Court would probably wish to have those directions made known, so that it would be clear to the public that they were acting under governmental direction and were not assuming responsibility. I can conceive circumstances where the Court or the Governors would regard that as satisfactory to their consciences and no further action was necessary. I can conceive cases which might involve resignations, either of the Governors or of the Court; but these are all those steps which are conceivable possibilities before one comes to that extreme point.

There were no published directions, or statement that

83

there had been no directions, after the trouble towards the end of 1964. Perhaps the Chancellor 'persuaded' the Governor to change his mind after Cromer recommended a rise in Bank Rate. Or perhaps there is a very significant difference between a 'positive directive' and a 'refusal to agree'. Whatever the exact position, it is clear that there does not need to be a 'direction' for the Chancellor of the Exchequer to have his own way. As Thorneycroft has written, 'Why direct any man when you have agreed what is to be done with him?' (1960, 13).

It was always possible during Cobbold's time as Governor, for the Court (represented by the Governor), and the Treasury (represented by the Chancellor in the last instance), to agree about the Bank Rate and credit policy decisions. Decisions about changes in the Bank Rate were agreed on each occasion. It was stated before the Radcliffe Committee that there have been occasions when there has been a delay in movement of the Bank Rate because of disagreement at some point between the Treasury and the Governor. But Makins told the Committee that, as far as he knew (in 1958), the Treasury had never at any time considered the issue of a direction to the Bank of England.

Most consultation is by informal discussion, within the Bank in the first instance, and between the Chancellor of the Exchequer and the Governor at another stage. Cobbold has said that it is not a regular practice to record such discussions, therefore if there had been an investigation about a change in policy in, for example, the last five years, we should have to rely for information about it, on the Governor's memory, aided by such papers as happened to have been written at the time. Lord Bridges has said that the Bank now expresses itself in writing a good deal more than it did, say, thirty years ago. But there seems plenty of evidence to agree with Samuel Brittan when he concluded that most of the real business between the Bank and the Treasury is done in conversation and less is put down on paper than anywhere else in Whitehall (Brittan, 1964, 60).

The present close relationship between the Bank and the Treasury is not so much the result of nationalisation as the result of the realisation that fiscal and monetary measures are complementary, and that the two should be related. That is why important changes in the Bank Rate have on recent occasions been announced on the same day and as part of a set of other measures to deal with the economic situation.

Policy is not made in the Treasury in quite the same way as in a government department concerned with formulating policy on expenditure or administering a social service. Sir Edmund Compton explained to the Radcliffe Committee that the difference is that in the Treasury (as in the Bank) it is formed at the top and handed down to a considerably greater extent than is the case in other departments. An example of this is the Budget: 'policy making on the Budget is done in a very small and high circle'.

Furthermore, whilst nationalisation may, outwardly, have reduced the independence of the Bank, in reality it may have increased its power to influence policy. This is because the Bank now has *ex officio* claim to representation on all kinds of committees at which the substance of Government economic policy is discussed and prepared; for example, a senior Bank of England official is now a member of the Treasury's Budget Committee (Brittan, 1964, 101).

During the Debate on the Monetary System in the House of Commons on November 26th, 1959, Heathcoat Amory, the Chancellor of the Exchequer, said he was sure it was known to every hon. Member that for very many years no change in the Bank Rate had been made without the approval of the Chancellor. But he then made it perfectly clear that a change in the Bank Rate is always made with the approval of the Chancellor of the Exchequer and explained the arrangements for the future:

> Broadly, the arrangements for the future—which I have of course, agreed with the Governor of the Bank of England—will be on the following lines. The Court of Directors has delegated to the Governor standing authority to settle changes in the Bank Rate with the Chancellor on behalf of the Bank. In framing the view of the Bank as to the level of the Bank Rate, the Governor will be free to have discussions with the Committee of Treasury and with other part-time directors of the Bank. He will not, however, put specific proposals before the Committee of Treasury or before the Court of Directors.
>
> When, following the customary informal discussions between the Governor and myself, a change in the Bank Rate is agreed to be desirable, the Governor will make a formal written proposal to me on the day before the change is to be made and I shall convey my approval in writing on the same day. The approval will cover both the change itself and the continuance of the Bank Rate at the new level until such time as a further change takes place. On the day on which the change is to be made, the Governor will report to the Court the action taken under the standing authority given to him. The final decision will be made in the name of the Bank and announced forthwith in the usual way.

The principle of unanimity

In the preparation for the decision the part-time directors (such as Kindersley and W. J. Keswick) played a very significant role.

For example, Kindersley, who had been travelling in the United States and Canada, returned on August 26th, three days earlier than he had intended, because he was so disturbed by the attitude of banking businessmen in Canada towards the pound sterling. On his return he saw Mynors on September 2nd and 12th, and they discussed in general terms the possibility of raising the Bank Rate. Not only did Kindersley come back to England with his recent experience of his visit to North America in mind, he was also in close touch with events in the City. He had early knowledge that the Vickers' issue was being underwritten. He had made contact with the 'preliminary feelers' which the underwriting businesses put out in the City. Kindersley was so close to the workings of the City that he felt it would be quite natural to approach Bicester (another part-time director of the Bank) and ask him whether the Vickers' issue could be stopped.

The role of the part-time directors was an important factor for the consideration of the Tribunal, but it is equally important from the point of view of how the decision was made. Clearly, the advice and guidance of such men who are so well aware of the City's activities is of great value to the Bank, but it also brings difficulties. It puts the directors themselves in a difficult position because their responsibilities to their companies means that they are expected to give them honest advice, but at the same time they must not, by any 'hint', disclose any special information they may have as directors of the Bank of England. This is not easy to do. All their friends and acquaintances know their position and may be willing to interpret any look or evasion as a 'hint'. Kindersley went to considerable lengths to avoid being approached for advice on subjects that might be related to the Bank Rate, but Lord Weeks told him later that he thought

Kindersley 'looked particularly "po-faced"' on September 18th.

The essence of this problem was probably put most clearly by Kindersley when he was asked by the Attorney-General: 'Is it right that you, or a director of the Bank of England should be exposed in this way?' and he replied: 'It is a very difficult question for me to answer; in fact, it is invidious for me to answer. It really boils down to this: is the contribution Lord Kindersley can make to the Bank of England worth the risk of his leaking a Bank Rate, or something like that?'

W. J. Keswick also recognised this as a very difficult position, for in his case he had a responsibility to give honest advice to Jardine, Matheson and Co, yet he also had a duty not to disclose anything directly or indirectly in relation to the Bank Rate.

There is, in decisions such as that to raise the Bank Rate, always a feeling of security in numbers. There is a preference for joint responsibility on important matters, and on a matter of such importance as a rise in the Bank Rate by two per cent, the Governor would certainly want to know that he had his Court with him. That was also why he wanted to clear away Kindersley's anxiety and was so willing for him to discuss the Vickers' issue with Bicester although he already knew that nothing could be done about it.

Cobbold told the Tribunal: 'It is quite invaluable for the Governor to be able to draw on this fund of knowledge and experience in formulating policy and to be able to share with the Court responsibility for decisions which must affect sterling throughout the world.' He also explained:

The normal practice when we are considering a specific

proposal like a change in the Bank Rate, is first to discuss those matters with the Committee of Treasury who are the recognised sub-committee of the Court for that purpose. My normal practice in addition to consulting and speaking to the Committee of Treasury, is in the first instance to get hold of those directors who seem best qualified to advise me on the particular matter in hand. The problem that we were facing at that moment was a major exchange crisis, and the directors whom I wished to consult in addition to the members of the Committee of Treasury, were those directors who were particularly qualified to give me an opinion about the likely effect of a seven per cent Bank Rate on sterling. Those directors, in addition to the members of the Committee of Treasury, were, in my opinion, Sir Charles Hambro, Mr Babington Smith and Lord Kindersley, and I therefore consulted them specifically first. . . .

Cobbold further explained to the Bank Rate Tribunal and to the Radcliffe Committee, that he sought unanimity on such questions as this. He said:

It is nice to be able to share one's responsibility with one's colleagues . . . I think it very much strengthens the position of the Governor and Deputy Governor in making those decisions for the world to know that they are made under the responsibility of such an experienced and widely based body of first class citizens. . . . I have in the course of my life to take a number of decisions on a number of different problems, and it is a great comfort to me that the responsibility is shared with others.

This is a good example of what Floyd Hunter, in his study *Community Power Structure*, has called 'the principle of unanimity in community work'. When a policy is finally formulated by the leaders of a community, there is an immediate demand on their part for strict conformity of opinion. Unanimity is sought, and pressure is put upon the dissenters before the project is really set going.

89

6

Some factors in decision making

The Attorney-General: As Governor of the Bank of
England and one of the Commissioners for the
Reduction of the National Debt, are you con-
cerned in stock transactions by these two bodies?
Mr Cobbold: I am.
The Attorney-General: In your capacity as
Governor of the Bank of England, you say you
are a trustee of a number of public, charitable
and other funds and also a member of the
governing body of Eton College?
Mr Cobbold: Yes.

(*Bank Rate Tribunal Evidence*)

The decision makers

It might be revealing to examine the backgrounds of all
the people involved in making this decision, but there is
the problem of which people should be considered as the
decision makers. The ideal may be to consider systematic-
ally each of the people who had knowledge of the decision
to raise the Bank Rate before the decision was publicly
announced. However, that can only be an ideal. It could
never be actually achieved because the people concerned
are not all known. We do know from the Minutes of
Evidence before the Tribunal that many people, including
many civil servants, whose names and positions, it is said,
cannot be revealed because of the confidential nature of

their advice, knew of the decision but were not called to give oral evidence at the Inquiry.

As the most important published material is the Minutes of Evidence, the criterion will be all those people who gave oral evidence at the Inquiry and who knew of the decision before the public announcement. Thirty-four people are in this category and there is published material (e.g. in *Who's Who*) about most of them.

First, consider education.

Of these thirty-four people, twenty-one were educated at major public schools ('Clarendon' schools), and nine of these twenty-one went to Eton. Eighteen went to Oxbridge (nine to Oxford University and nine to Cambridge University).

In examining these figures there are some qualifications to be noted. Information about schools attended is published for only thirty of the thirty-four. On the subject of universities attended it should be remembered that many of these people have entered a family business on leaving school, and a university career may not have been considered as valuable for their ultimate careers as training inside the business itself. Again, whilst eighteen went to Oxbridge and only two attended another university, it must be remembered that the average date of birth of these men was 1902 and therefore when they were of undergraduate age there would have been few alternatives to Oxford and Cambridge for a university education.

However, certain conclusions may still be drawn from these figures. For even after making these qualifications, the large proportion of these people who have been educated at Eton (nine out of thirty) and Oxbridge (eighteen out of thirty) means that they were drawn from a distinctive group in society, and this gives them certain advantages from the standpoint of common attitudes and

91

makes communication between them easy. But these factors are hardly surprising when it is realised how people like directors of the Bank of England are appointed. Cobbold, who, in his capacity as Governor of the Bank of England, was also a governor of Eton, explained to the Tribunal that the Chancellor of the Exchequer always discussed such appointments with him when he was Governor of the Bank, and added that it was 'absolutely unthinkable' that somebody who had not got a record of complete integrity should ever be considered.

Secondly, consider club memberships.

If the total club memberships of these people are analysed, remembering that one person is often a member of more than one club, the most popular clubs are: Carlton (6), White's (5), Atheneum (5), Boodle's (4), Brooks' (4), Union (3), Pratt's (3), M.C.C. (3), Turf (2), United University (2).

Club memberships may be an important factor in decision-making because they provide considerable opportunity for frequent informal contact. They may also contribute to the perpetuation of an élite or ruling class because they are, by nature, closed communities.

Thirdly, consider how certain members of the group are related by marriage and business.

Cobbold, then Governor of the Bank of England, is a member of a family of landed gentry. He is related on his father's side to the late Lt. Col. John Cobbold, who married a daughter of the 9th Duke of Devonshire. Lt. Col. Cobbold's sister married Sir Charles Hambro, a Director of the Bank of England, and Lt. Col. H. E. Hambro married the widow of the 5th Earl of Cadogan, whose grandson married a daughter of Lt. Col. Cobbold. Lady Dorothy Macmillan, who was a daughter of the 9th Duke of Devonshire, and wife of the Prime Minister, was therefore sister-in-law to Lt. Col. John Cobbold. Cobbold is now Lord Chamberlain and a director of British Petroleum, Royal Exchange Assurance, Hudson's Bay Company and other companies.

M. J. Babington Smith, a Director of the Bank of England, married a daughter of Admiral Hon. Herbert Meade-Fetherstonhaugh, and is thus connected by marriage to the Glyn banking family. Babington Smith is a director of Glyn Mills and Co, Associated Electrical Industries Ltd, and other companies.

The 11th Duke of Devonshire, nephew by marriage of Macmillan, is brother-in-law of the writer Nancy Mitford; she married a son of Lord Rennell. Lord Rennell's wife is a sister of the late Lord Bicester, a senior Director of Morgan Grenfell and Co, and Director of the Bank of England (Lord Bicester was the 'Rufie' referred to in the Evidence). Lord Rennell is also connected to the Keswick family by the marriage of his sister to a brother-in-law of J. H. Keswick.

Mynors, then Deputy Governor of the Bank of England, is descended on his mother's side from a sister of Mr J. Spender Clay. His brother, and the Earl of Home (now Sir Alec Douglas Home), then Secretary of State for Commonwealth Relations, married sisters, members of the Lyttleton family. The son of Lord Chandos (Oliver Lyttleton) married the daughter of Sir Alan Lascelles, brother-in-law of the 1st Lord Lloyd. Mynors is also related to the Brand family (of Lazards) and, more distantly, to the Colvilles of Rothschilds.

Nigel Birch married a daughter of the 4th Baron Wolverton whose wife was a sister of the 2nd Earl of Dudley. Birch was the Economic Secretary to the Treasury and a member of the Keswick shooting party (which also included a member of the Hambro family) mentioned in the Evidence.

Kindersley, a Director of the Bank of England, is brother-in-law to a niece of the 2nd Earl of Iveagh, and father-in-law of Lord Boyd (then the Rt. Hon. Alan Lennox-Boyd, Secretary of State for Colonial Affairs). The Earl of Iveagh is also father-in-law to a sister of the Rt. Hon. John Hare, M.P. (now Lord Blakenham) whose wife is a sister to Viscount Cowdray, who was mentioned in the Evidence in connection with the Pearson Group of Companies. (Lazards is part of the Pearson Group, and Poole became Chairman of Lazards at the beginning of 1966. It was for an executive directorship in S. Pearson and Co. Ltd, that F. A. Bishop left the civil service in September 1965. Bishop was at the time of the Bank Rate decision Principal Private Secretary to the Prime Minister, and at the time of leaving the civil service Permanent Secretary to the Ministry of Land and Natural Resources.)

Since leaving the civil service Sir Leslie Rowan has become Chairman of Vickers, and Makins is now Chairman of Hill, Samuel, the merchant bankers.

Fourthly, consider the team spirit that existed among these decision makers.

This team spirit is particularly to be found in the City, where much of the business is done 'on trust'. The City itself is a relatively small, tightly organised, closely knit community, and Cobbold once said, whilst Governor of the Bank of England, 'if I want(ed) to talk to the representatives of the . . . whole financial community, we (could) usually get together in one room in about half an hour' (Grove, 1962, 447). Kindersley talked to the Tribunal about 'putting out feelers', and agreed that 'sub-underwriting is a sort of club'. He also said: '. . . had I realised that Morgans had signed the contract, that the sub-underwriters had undertaken their sub-underwriting, I would no more have suggested cancelling that Vickers' issue than

94

fly over the moon, because the City does not do that sort of thing; you are committed.' Similarly, R. H. Fry, Financial Editor of the *Manchester Guardian* explained to the Tribunal that the City relies completely on information that comes from trustworthy persons.

But while this aura of trust may be very useful for the way the City operates, it may at the same time be spreading an attitude of complacent acceptance.

The Bank Rate was raised on September 19th, and from 20th there were rumours in the press about 'inspired selling' and 'a Bank Rate Leak'. But the Governor of the Bank of England did not take the press statements very seriously because they were not confirmed by anything he heard from other quarters at the time. He therefore made no inquiry about the rumours until, on the 25th, the Treasury rang up the Bank and said there was a meeting fixed for that morning and asked if the Bank would be represented. As a result, the Governor went to see the Financial Secretary.

Consequently, at 11.40 that morning the Governor left a document with the Financial Secretary in which he said 'Although I have heard one or two rumours since the event, that some Press or other people had prior information about the Bank Rate, I do not myself feel that there is any *prima facie* evidence of a leakage about Bank Rate, nor have I heard any serious suggestion in the City that there was.' But it was not until September 26th, a week after the Bank Rate was raised, that Cobbold spoke to Kindersley and Keswick about the matter.

Cobbold told the Tribunal that he thought 'that if the Prime Minister had wanted to know about it he would ask me and the immediate question he would ask would be "You are the Governor: I want to know whether you are satisfied on this"'.

After reading the Evidence one may well come to the conclusion that whilst there is a very useful place for such trust and integrity, the people who are in the highest positions should, on occasions such as that, carry out the most rigorous investigations and rely less on feelings and trust. Even as late as December 16th 1957, Cobbold was still telling the Tribunal 'I have not seen the list of detailed Stock Exchange transactions'. Such statements show both the Governor's feelings and the Lord Chancellor's 'investigation' in a rather unfavourable light. Yet the Lord Chancellor's investigation was described by the Prime Minister on November 14th as 'a most careful and searching inquiry into every aspect of the evidence produced and down every path to which that evidence might lead'. He did not add that the searching inquiry did not even include the Governor of the Bank of England finding out about Stock Exchange transactions.

Fifthly, consider the honours that have been bestowed on the decision makers since 1957.

This is interesting because one of the most obvious facts about any given circle of men is the criteria of praise, of honour and position that prevails among them. In this case the following are the most significant examples:

The decision makers and others closely connected with the case study:

Mr C. F. Cobbold—Lord Cobbold (Baron cr. 1958)
Mr G. Eley—Sir Geoffrey Eley (Kt. 1964)
Sir Roger Makins—Lord Sherfield (1st Baron cr. 1964)
Professor L. Robbins—Lord Robbins (Baron cr. 1959)
Mr W. J. Mullens—Sir William Mullens (Kt. 1963)
Mr H. Mynors—Sir Humphrey Mynors (1st Bt. cr. 1964)
Mr M. H. Parsons—Sir Maurice Parsons (Kt. 1966)
Sir Harry Pilkington—Lord Pilkington (Baron cr. 1968)
Lord Mills (Baron)—Viscount Mills (1st Viscount cr. 1962)

Mr B. Sanderson—Lord Sanderson (1st Baron cr. 1960)
Mr Peter Thorneycroft—Lord Thorneycroft (Baron cr. 1967)
Sir Oliver Franks—Lord Franks (Baron cr. 1962)
Mr R. M. Fraser—Sir Richard Fraser (Kt. 1958)
Mr E. Milner Holland—Sir Edward Milner Holland (Kt. 1959)
Dr Charles Hill—Lord Hill (Baron cr. 1963)
Sir Reginald Manningham Buller—Lord Dilhorne (Baron cr. 1962, 1st Viscount cr. 1964)
Mr G. Newton—Sir Gordon Newton (Kt. 1966)
Lord Justice Parker—Lord Chief Justice Parker (Baron cr. 1958)
Mr Oliver Poole—Lord Poole (1st Baron cr. 1958)

It is not suggested that there is anything sinister about the honours that these people have received. Clearly they are the sort of people who are in responsible positions and who could reasonably expect to be so rewarded. However, it may be that the granting of these honours does not necessarily signify bestowing a reward. Also, it may be that the most interesting feature of this aspect of the case is not so much noticing the people who have been honoured, as the people who *have not*.

Furthermore, the giving of honours may also indicate a condition of good relations between the institutions and persons involved in government. For example, when Parsons received his knighthood in the New Year's honours in 1966, *The Times* commented: 'In Government circles yesterday it was being said that this reward was an indication of the good relations that now exist between the Government and the City.'

Holidays

In an examination of decision making, each factor contributing to the decision must be considered both in itself and in its relationship to other factors. It is only in this way, by seeing the whole situation, that a clear picture can emerge of how the decision was made.

One of the most significant factors in the Bank Rate decision was the holiday period. Holidays are important in any advanced society, but it may be more than an interesting coincidence that the 1936 Budget Leak Tribunal was investigating the events over a holiday period (Easter) and in 1957 the summer holiday period had a significant effect on the Bank Rate decision.

On August 7th the Chancellor of the Exchequer gave specific instructions for the Treasury to study the possibility of bringing about a measure of deflation in the economy. He then went on holiday abroad.

The Governor of the Bank of England attended the regular Thursday morning meetings of the Bank's Court of Directors on August 7th, 14th and 21st, then he left England for a holiday abroad from August 24th to September 14th. Consequently, Mynors deputised for him at the meeting of the Bank's Committee of Treasury on August 28th, and told the Committee that the Bank Rate had not come under discussion with the Treasury but that he was keeping it under review.

Makins went on leave from August 29th to September 5th, then on September 6th he had lunch at the Bank of England.

Sometime during this period Professor Lionel Robbins, who was on holiday in Switzerland, was telephoned by Thorneycroft, who asked him to come back to London.

Then, during the week following September 9th, Thorneycroft had some preliminary discussion with the Deputy Governor of the Bank about the possibility of raising the Bank Rate, but they thought it better to defer any definite discussion until after the Governor himself had returned from holiday on the 15th or 16th.

Mynors had called on Makins at the Treasury on September 12th, and they discussed the contents of the draft statement to be made by the Chancellor the following week. Mynors said he would be prepared to discuss the question of raising the Bank Rate with the Chancellor next day, but that any recommendation to the Court would have to await the return of the Governor.

On September 14th Cobbold returned from his holiday and immediately went to see Mynors at his house in the country, and Mynors brought the Governor up to date with the developments during the three weeks of his holiday.

It is therefore not surprising that Mynors explained to the Tribunal that 'It was an exceptionally difficult situation, I think, partly because of the holiday season. If certain people had returned earlier from holiday these things would have been spread over a longer period and begun earlier.' But it makes one wonder what would have happened had there been no holidays—one might have thought that no holidays would have meant less delays rather than involving a longer period of time. Perhaps it may not have been unreasonable to expect that some of the people who were in posts of exceptional responsibility should have postponed their holidays because of the seriousness of the situation.

Kindersley returned from Canada on August 24th, three days earlier than he had intended, because he was 'really worried' by the attitude of Canadian bankers, and indeed, of all Canadian businessmen, 'towards the pound sterling in general, towards our inability to stop the wage spiral, and our ineffective . . . Government at the time'.

Mr C. A. S. Cooper, the Investment Secretary of the

99

Royal Exchange Assurance, broke his holiday on August 28th in order to meet Kindersley who had just returned after his six weeks in North America, then Cooper resumed his holiday and finally returned to work on September 16th.

Mr T. H. Brand, one of the Managing Directors of Lazards for over twenty-six years, who had been to Norway, returned to England on September 9th and he told the Tribunal that it was certainly noticeable to him when he returned, that foreign deposits at Lazards were falling rather badly, and he drew attention to this at the money day meeting at Lazards on Friday 13th September.

W. J. Keswick, a Director of the Bank of England, was on his shooting holiday in Scotland when he received the letter from the Deputy Governor about the measures that might be taken to deal with the exchange situation, including possible action on the Bank Rate.

When these facts are considered, and the reactions of the various people when they assessed the economic situation after their holidays, it seems that there are two reasons why holidays played an important role in this decision.

The first concerns delays. It was not until Monday, September 16th, when many of these people had returned from their holidays, that it was possible to proceed with the process leading up to the decision. The question remains of whether action was unnecessarily delayed during this holiday period, and it needs to be asked whether there was sufficient delegation of authority while so many of the country's top administrators took holidays. Why, for example, when Cobbold has specifically said that the Deputy Governor has the full authority of the Governor, in his absence, was Mynors so emphatic about deferring definite discussion about the Bank Rate until the Governor had returned from his holiday? Why did none of these people in posts of top responsibility postpone their holidays in the light of the very serious economic situation?

There is something more than slightly incongruous in a situation like this in the twentieth century. Is it really necessary that the whole administrative and productive tempo of the country should almost shut down for a specific period of summer holidays? Little thought seems to have been given to this aspect of the problem. Even the official surveys on the subject of holidays have been more concerned with the tourist trade than with the welfare of the country's economy. If the experience and views of the Governor of the Bank of England were so important why was he not recalled from his holiday? It will be remembered that Robbins was called back to London from Switzerland to advise Thorneycroft, and Macmillan cancelled his holiday in Scotland.

The facts suggest there is a certain procedural pattern observed in such matters as the raising of the Bank Rate. Everyone concerned in the decision making was aware of this and seems to have had an inflexible attitude towards it. In this pattern there were clearly recognisable roles to be played by the Governor, the Chancellor, the Directors of the Bank and others. In 1957 the pattern was so established that when the holiday period meant the decision-making circle was broken, the procedure was interrupted until the circle was again complete.

But it is not only a question of interrupting a procedural pattern. These holidays were probably also important because they interrupted the formation of concensus, which increases the significance of, and authority behind, decisions. It gives comfort to the decision makers who feel that what they decide will then be accepted, and it may even influence some aspects of the decision itself. It is therefore suggested that the holidays in 1957 were significant in the decision making process because they interrupted the established procedure, which in turn may have caused the decision makers to feel insecure and disinclined to reach a conclusion until as many people as possible had been prepared for the decision.

Secondly, holidays are important because of their relationship to changes of attitude. They are sometimes a factor in bringing together, or interrelating, different attitude groups. W. J. Keswick put this succinctly in another context when he told the Tribunal: 'The more you are outside the United Kingdom looking in, the worse does devaluation look.'

Holiday changes benefit people in authority in two ways. They are able to make contact with new people (as Kindersley did when talking to the Canadian businessmen). They also enable people to see the situation from a more detached viewpoint, they have time for reflection and can consider the position afresh, and when they return to work they see old problems in a new light. Such changes enable decision makers to widen their experience as well as provide opportunities for refreshment and recreation.

Communication and consensus

Once the decision was made, it was important to ensure the success of the policy by communicating the decision and the reasoning behind it to everyone involved.

In addition to the Directors of the Bank of England, members of the Bank's permanent staff such as the Chief Cashier, Secretary and Deputy Secretary and certain senior officials already knew of the decision. Other people who knew included the Governor's private secretary, the private secretaries to the Deputy Governor and Chief Cashier and personal typists and filing clerks. It was also necessary for the proper functioning of the Bank that the decision should be communicated to others, including the Government Broker and the Controller of the National Debt Office.

In addition, there were the people who were informed of the 'other measures' that were being effected (that is, the economic measures apart from the change in the Bank Rate).

Lord Mills, then Minister of Power, saw Lord Citrine, Sir Christopher Hinton, Sir Henry Self, Sir Henry Jones and Sir James Bowman. They were all heads of nationalised industries.

Mr Ian Macleod, then Minister of Labour and National Service, saw representatives of the Trades Union Congress (Sir Vincent Tewson, Sir Tom Williamson and Mr T. Yates) and representatives of the British Employers' Confederation (Sir Colin Anderson and Mr Pollock).

Thorneycroft saw Poole, Fraser and Dear from the Conservative Party, Moore, Tyerman, Bareau, McLachlan and Gampbell from the newspapers, and Kipping, the Director-General of the Federation of British Industries.

The Cabinet felt it was necessary that these people should be told. The chairmen of the nationalised industries were told because it was thought that it would be discourteous to allow them to discover the first news of the measures affecting their industries from the press. The representatives of the T.U.C. and the Employers were told because Parliament was not sitting at the time. If it had been, then it would have been possible for a statement to have been made by the Chancellor in the House of Commons.

Another reason for seeing such people as the representatives was that it was felt that it would encourage support for the Government's policy. The pressure on the pound was really basically due to the belief at home and abroad that there was an inflationary condition with which the Government were not dealing, and Thorneycroft felt that failure in any of those quarters to understand the purpose or significance of his statement might well have imperilled the whole operation. It would certainly have gravely weakened Thorneycroft's position at the meeting of the International Monetary Fund.

However, these communications also contributed to an atmosphere, consensus, or will. As Mr Daniel Meinertzhagen, a Managing Director of Lazards, put it in his evidence before the Tribunal, 'one feels there is a crisis or emergency about'. The publication of the reserves' figures also contributed to this—225 million dollars of reserves were lost by Britain during August and these figures were published on September 5th. There was the thought in people's minds all over the world, not just in this country, that the deutschmark was likely to be revalued. The significant role of the press in these matters was emphasised by Mr J. K. K. Pennefather, a broker who told the Tribunal that 'in our profession we do read what the Financial Editors and other financial scribes do write and it is apt to influence us in decisions and suggest views'.

An administrative process

Although it is often difficult in public administration to decide where policy ends and administration begins, and attempts to differentiate between the two are constantly becoming invalid, it may be said that the decision to raise the Bank Rate by two per cent in 1957 was such a significant decision of administration that it became a decision of policy. One wonders, for example, whether any of these problems of responsibility and consultation would have arisen if it had been decided to raise the Bank Rate, not by two per cent but by one per cent (Cooper, the Investment Secretary of the Royal Exchange Assurance, thought the Bank Rate ought to have been raised to six per cent at least a month earlier). One wonders who it was who decided it should be *two* per cent (the Minutes of Evidence before the Tribunal suggest that it was the Governor who decided that the rate be raised by *two* per cent, but there is no indication of where he got his idea from). This particular aspect was not, of course, one that concerned the Tribunal, but there were other problems that were not primarily the concern of the Tribunal, about which we now know a great deal. It is a little surprising that there was no mention in the Evidence of any discussion about the size of the increase in the Bank Rate.

In this context, Cobbold explained to the Tribunal that his primary concern was:

> was a rather sensational rise in the Bank Rate from five per cent to seven per cent likely to be a really effec-
> tive measure along with the other measures under con-
> sideration—which in my judgement it was—or was
> there a risk that such a sensational measure as a two
> per cent rise from five to seven per cent might be
> regarded on the exchanges as some sort of panic action?

The constitutional test of a government decision may be whether it would be acceptable to Parliament, but it is usual for Parliament to accept a decision of the Cabinet or a decision that has been approved by the Cabinet: indeed, one of the functions of the Cabinet is the final determination of the policy to be submitted to Parliament. On this occasion the Cabinet were told at their meeting on Tuesday, September 17th, that 'by tradition' (why 'by tradition', surely it was by law?) a decision on the Bank Rate was not their responsibility. The Cabinet agreed that the point should be left for further discussion by the Prime Minister, the Chancellor of the Exchequer and the Governor of the Bank of England. On Bank Rate day the Cabinet were informed that the Prime Minister had reached the conclusion that the Government should accept the view of the Bank of England that the Bank Rate should be increased to seven per cent, and the Cabinet took note of that decision. The evidence suggests that no other member of the Cabinet was consulted before the decision was reached. It concerned only the Chancellor of the Exchequer and the Prime Minister.

Furthermore, it was normal practice, in the event of a proposed change, for the Governors to ascertain whether the Chancellor would agree before they made the proposal to the Committee of Treasury on the Wednesday morning. This meant that they would see whether the Chancellor would agree with something that was not really his responsibility. Such a situation makes it even more difficult to see any division between politics and administration.

Frank J. Goodnow asserted that certain processes of government were concerned solely with the formulation of the will of the state—these he called policy processes—while others were concerned with the execution of that will—the administrative processes. It was a corollary of this doctrine that as administration was only the instrument of policy, because its goals were determined for it by the legislative body, its success could be judged entirely in terms of efficiency.

H. A. Simon, recalling the words of Goodnow, has said that as long as the government administrator was treated as a mere instrument of policy, administrative theory did not need to be much concerned with his characteristics as a human being. But Simon has found that administrative departments and the people in them may have goals of their own. They constitute a group which may have its own will. It would be interesting to know whether Cobbold, consciously or unconsciously, felt that he was protecting his group by saying that he was satisfied there was no need for an investigation even before he had made any proper inquiries. There are psychological characteristics of administrators about which it would be interesting to know more (Simon, 1955).

In another sense it may be argued that political forces and trends made the Bank Rate decision inevitable. Whether the Bank Rate is altered or not depends on the conditions of the time. But given the unfavourable conditions of the summer of 1957, the fact that the Government and the Bank took no action meant that conditions deteriorated until the situation was reached where a rise in the Bank Rate was inevitable if devaluation was to be averted. Perhaps one could say that there were in fact two decisions. The first was the decision to do nothing (July, August, first part of September) in which the delays caused by holidays were important, (there is a tendency for a proposal for no action to be more readily accepted all along the line as against ten others advocating some sort of positive move). It might be argued that the delay itself fulfilled an important function; for delay is sometimes an alternative to refusing a request when acceptance may lead to an open expression of conflict. Conflict may damage not only friendships, but also family relationships, and family relationships must be considered in any study of the working of the City. The second decision was the decision to raise the Bank Rate.

This study reveals how authority was accumulated in making the decision, and also the considerable personal authority possessed by the Governor of the Bank of England.

Indeed, Cobbold's personal authority as Governor of the Bank at that time is particularly significant. The nominal value of the total transactions made just before the announcement of the rise in the Bank Rate by the Matheson Group, the Royal Exchange and Lazards was about £4¼ million. Cobbold told the Tribunal that although he regarded the total as large, it was 'perfectly reasonable and explicable'. This was a remarkable statement. Few men in positions of such responsibility could state that transactions of such size were perfectly reasonable and entirely explicable before they had even made enquiries about them (and Cobbold made this statement to the Prime Minister on the 25th although he did not himself make any enquiries until the 26th or 27th).

The authority Cobbold felt he had in these circumstances is revealed by his answers to questions put to him by the Attorney-General. Cobbold said: 'I would have thought that the Prime Minister would wish to know whether I was satisfied that there was no irregularity, and the point to me appeared irrelevant whether it was for £10,000 or £1,000,000 or £5,000,000'. Later, the Attorney-General asked him: '. . . you merely told the Prime Minister that you would supply details, but you, as Governor of the Bank of England, were absolutely confident, in the three instances which had come to your ears, that everything was entirely proper and that there was no question of any irregularity whatever?' Cobbold replied: 'That is so.' The most important aspect of this seems to be not so much the size of the transaction, but that a man in the position of Governor of the Bank of England, who felt that his role was to tell the Prime Minister whether he was satisfied about a particular matter, could do so without making any proper investigation.

The accumulation of authority also depended on consultation with everyone concerned. There was a sense of security in involving the maximum number of important people. Two outstanding examples illustrate this. First, Thorneycroft and Mynors decided to defer any definite discussion about the Bank Rate until after the Governor had returned from his holiday (this was in spite of the very grave economic situation and although the Deputy Governor has full authority when the Governor is away). Secondly, when Kindersley asked Cobbold whether it was possible to postpone the Bank Rate rise until the Chancellor of the Exchequer had gone to the I.M.F. meeting, Cobbold replied that it could not be postponed until then because 'practically every Cabinet Minister in the place would be in Canada or America'. Yet the only members of the Cabinet involved in this decision were the Prime Minister and the Chancellor.

These consultations led to the formation of a consensus, but there is a way in which the usual notion of consensus can be inverted in administration. Usually, when we speak of consensus, we refer to the general attitude or will on a particular matter, a form of pressure which may influence the government. The characteristic procedure associated with this notion is to look for a consensus among the relevant interest groups and then to translate the consensus into policy and action. The significance of consensus may be increased if the procedure is inverted, and this seems to be what happened in September 1957.

Instead of looking for a consensus, the decision makers, recognising its significance for their authority, set out to create it by consulting and informing as many people as possible. The Chancellor and Governor were practising a technique for achieving consensus through the many consultations that took place, and there are two aspects of this procedure which seem important from the standpoint of the accumulation of authority. The first aspect concerns the role of the decision makers, and the second concerns pluralism.

As far as the decision makers are concerned, it may be said that they were seeking to create a consensus to add to their authority because they felt particularly anxious and insecure. This is not necessarily a poor reflection on the persons concerned but it is a reflection on the nature of authority. It may not be in the least surprising that the decision makers felt anxious and insecure in 1957, for they were raising the Bank Rate to its highest level for thirty-seven years and making the biggest rise in Bank Rate in peace time since 1847. It may not be at all surprising that while their positions gave the Chancellor and Governor *formal* authority, they wanted to maximise their *real* authority by creating a consensus of support. In this way the importance of consensus may be to confer on the decisions of the administrators a higher degree of authority than they would otherwise have.

As far as the pluralistic aspect of authority is concerned, it seems that those involved (and particularly the Chancellor and the Governor) were seeking to draw into the consensus as many interests as possible; they were not concerned with *why* people were supporting them, they were concerned that they had the maximum possible support. Thus, Cobbold wanted to make sure he had Kindersley's support; similarly, the Government went out of its way to make sure that the chairmen of the major nationalised industries and press representatives were kept informed of the other measures. The people concerned had to be convinced that they should support the decision, they had to be persuaded that a two per cent increase in the Bank Rate was in their interest because it was in the general interest of the country.

The Governor appears in this decision as the centre of a web of interaction. He had intimate knowledge of his Court of Directors otherwise they would not have been appointed. He also originated interaction between the Bank and the Treasury by formulating a decision that he was confident would be obeyed. It may be argued that the Deputy Governor, as deputy, did not have the status to back up his authority—whilst he appeared to have the authority it was not effective authority (he waited for the Governor to return from holiday).

There are two other ways of looking at the communications that took place and the formulation of the decision in 1957. They may be called the principle of unanimity and the absence of the collective idea. From his study *Community Power Structure*, Floyd Hunter was impressed by what he called 'the principle of unanimity'. By that he meant that when policy is finally formulated by the leaders in a community, there is an immediate demand on their part for strict conformity of opinion. Because decisions are not usually arrived at hurriedly, there is ample time for discussion before a stage for action is set. But when the time for discussion is past and the line is set, then unanimity is called for.

There is evidence in the 1957 Bank Rate decision to support Hunter's hypotheses. There were several weeks between August 7th when the Chancellor first gave his instructions to the Treasury, and September 15th, when the Governor returned from his holiday. This was the period of the 'formal dance'. Discussion was continuing in the Treasury, the Bank, the newspapers and the City. But when the stage was set, and the almost magical figure of two per cent had been selected, then it was unanimity that was required.

When the discussions with the Chancellor had taken

place Cobbold was not so much concerned with seeking the advice of the other members of the Court as making sure that they would not upset his plans. He had to think how awkward it would be if, at the meeting of the Court (the body which he consistently claimed made the decision) someone were to say that he did not agree with it. It might have been very interesting if someone had said at the Court that he thought the increase should have been to six per cent rather than seven per cent. It seems that the organisation of the Bank is designed not so much to discuss general policy as to implement or approve policies handed down from above.

Cobbold explained that his normal practice was to get hold of those directors who seemed best qualified to advise him on the particular matter in hand. He explained that in September 1957, those directors, in addition to members of the Committee of Treasury, were Hambro, Babington Smith and Kindersley, and he therefore consulted them first. But he also explained that the particular matter in hand was 'the likely effect of a seven per cent Bank rise on sterling'—not whether seven per cent would be appropriate. Even at that stage, it was no longer a question of *whether*.

It is also interesting that Cobbold saw all but one of the members of the Court before the meeting. Perhaps a majority would have been enough to carry the decision, but he wanted the security of numbers, the security of unanimity.

This means that Cobbold's consultations were not intended to draw out a collective idea but to ensure that there was uniformity. Cobbold's reason for agreeing that Kindersley should consult Bicester was that he would then agree to the decision that had already been reached. On the other hand, Kindersley's reason for wanting to see

Bicester was to see whether any alternative decision (not only on the Bank Rate, but on the Vickers' issue) was still possible. There is therefore less evidence to suggest the drawing out of a collective idea than there is to support the demand for uniformity after the somewhat magical decision was reached.

An examination of the details of such a case as this suggests that there is no one, clear, administrative process. Administration is much more complex than that. There may be certain common characteristics in various cases, but each case is separate, it is something quite different from each other case. And one of the reasons for this is that the people involved in the case are human beings, and human nature is an important factor in administration. The Bank Rate decision of 1957 may have been quite different if Cobbold had not been the Governor of the Bank of England, if Macmillan had not been the Prime Minister, or indeed, if there had been any other changes in the cast.

Bibliography and guide to further reading

A. *Source works (from which the case study in this monograph has been constructed)*

Proceedings of the Tribunal appointed to Inquire into Allegations that information about the raising of the Bank Rate was improperly disclosed, with Minutes of Evidence taken before the Tribunal. H.M.S.O., 1957.

Report of the Tribunal to Inquire into Allegations of Improper Disclosure relating to the Raising of the Bank Rate. (Cmnd 350), H.M.S.O., 1958.

B. *Other official papers and Reports*

Report of the Committee on the Working of the Monetary System. (Cmnd 827), H.M.S.O., 1960.
This is the report of the Radcliffe Committee.

Committee on the Working of the Monetary System, Memoranda and Evidence (3 vols.). H.M.S.O., 1960.
Vol. 1 contains memoranda from the Treasury and the Bank of England, vol. 3 contains evidence by top administrators at the Treasury and the Bank, also evidence by leading politicians on the working of the monetary system.

Minutes of Evidence taken before the Tribunal appointed under the Tribunals of Inquiry Act, 1921, The Budget Disclosure Inquiry, 1936. H.M.S.O., 1936.
Contains useful evidence on the working of the Cabinet by Sir Maurice Hankey, Secretary to the Cabinet for nearly twenty years, also evidence by Sir Norman Fisher, Permanent Secretary to the Treasury and Head of the Civil Service.

Minutes of Evidence taken in London before the Royal Commission on Indian Currency and Finance. H.M.S.O., 1926.
Contains evidence by The Rt Hon. Montagu Norman, Governor of the Bank of England, on relations between the Bank and the Government.

115

Minutes of Evidence before the Committee on Finance and Industry. H.M.S.O., 1931.
The evidence before the Macmillan Committee.

Staggered Holidays. (Cmnd 2105) H.M.S.O., 1963.
The White Paper from the Board of Trade which analyses the British holiday season.

C. *Works with special reference to the 1957 decision, the Cabinet and the City*

BRITTAN, SAMUEL (1964), *The Treasury Under the Tories 1951-1964*, Penguin Books.
DEVONS, ELY, 'An Economist's View of the Bank Rate Tribunal Evidence', *The Manchester School of Economics and Social Studies*, xxvii (1959), 1-16.
FERRIS, PAUL (1962), *The City*, Penguin Books.
HANHAM, H. J., 'A Political Scientist's View of the Bank Rate Tribunal Evidence', *The Manchester School of Economic and Social Studies*, xxvii (1959), 17-29.
HOBSON, SIR OSCAR, 'As I See It . . .' *The Banker*, cviii (1958), 24-28.
KEETON, GEORGE W. (1960), *Trial by Tribunal*, Museum Press.
MACKINTOSH, JOHN P. (1962), *The British Cabinet*, Stevens.
ROBBINS, LIONEL, 'Thoughts on the Crisis', *Lloyds Bank Review*, New Series, xlviii (1958), 1-26.
THE BANKER, 'The Bank of England from Within', *The Banker*, cviii (1958), 162-171.
WILSON, C. SHIRLEY and T. LUPTON, 'The Social Background and Connections of "Top Decision-Makers"', *The Manchester School of Economic and Social Studies*, xxvii (1959), 30-51.

D. *Works with special reference to decision-making theory, élites, groups, etc.*

AARONOVITCH, S. (1961), *The Ruling Class*, Lawrence and Wishart.
A.S.A. monographs 2 (1965), *Political Systems and the Distribution of Power*, Tavistock.
BAKER, R. J. S., 'Discussion and Decision-Making in the Civil Service', *Public Administration*, xli (1963), 345-356.
BARNARD, CHESTER I. (1938), *The Functions of the Executive*, Cambridge, Mass.: Harvard University Press.
BENTLEY, ARTHUR F. (1908), *The Process of Government*, Bloomington, Indiana: The Principia Press.
BEVERIDGE, LORD (1958), *Power and Influence*, New York: Beechurst Press.
BOTTOMORE, T. B. (1964), *Elites and Society*, Watts.

CHAPMAN, BRIAN (1963), *British Government Observed*, Allen and Unwin.

DAALDER, HANS, 'The Haldane Committee and the Cabinet', *Public Administration*, xli (1963), 117-135.

DAHL, ROBERT A. (1961), *Who Governs?*, Yale University Press.

DIMOCK, MARSHALL E. (1958), *A Philosophy of Administration*, New York: Harper and Row.

FOLLETT, M. P. (1949), *Freedom and Co-ordination*, Management Publications Trust.

GORE, WILLIAM J. and FREDERICK S. SILANDER, 'A Bibliographical Essay on Decision-Making', *Administrative Science Quarterly*, iv (1959-60), 97-120.

GROVE, J. (1962), *Government and Industry in Britain*, Longmans.

GUTTSMAN, W. L. (1963), *The British Political Elite*, MacGibbon & Kee.

HUNTER, FLOYD (1963), *Community Power Structure—A Study of Decision Makers*, Chapel Hill: North Carolina University Press.

MARVICK, DWAINE (editor) (1961), *Political Decision-Makers*, Glencoe: The Free Press.

MATTHEWS, DONALD R. (1954), *The Social Background of Political Decision-Makers*, New York: Doubleday.

MILLS, C. WRIGHT (1956), *The Power Elite*, New York: Oxford University Press.

NETTL, J. P., 'Consensus or Elite Domination: The Case of Business', *Political Studies*, xiii (1965), 22-44.

PFIFFNER, JOHN M. and R. V. PRESTHUS (1960), *Public Administration*, New York: Ronald.

RHODES, GERALD (1965), *Administrators in Action, Vol. II*, Allen and Unwin.

ROBSON, W. A., 'Teaching and Research in Public Administration', *Public Administration*, xxxix (1961), 217-222.

SIMON, H. A. (1955), 'Recent Advances in Organisation Theory' in *Research Frontiers in Politics and Government*, Washington: Brookings Institution.

SNYDER, RICHARD C. and GLENN D. PAIGE, 'The United States Decision to Resist Aggression in Korea, The Application of an Analytical Scheme', *Administrative Science Quarterly*, iii (1958-59), 341-378.

WADE, H. W. R. (1961), *Administrative Law*, Oxford University Press, (Clarendon Law Series).

WALLAS, GRAHAM (reprinted 1948), *Human Nature in Politics*, Constable.

WILSON, F. M. G. (1961), *Administrators in Action*, Vol. I, Allen and Unwin.

E. Works with special reference to the organisation of the Bank of England and the Treasury.

ANDRÉADES, A. (1909), *History of the Bank of England*, P. S. King and Son.

BAGEHOT, WALTER (reprinted 1917), *Lombard Street, A Description of the Money Market*, John Murray.

BAREAU, PAUL, 'An Outside View', in *The Bank of England Today*, The Institute of Banker's Sykes Memorial Lectures, 1964.

BEAVERBROOK, LORD (1965), *Men and Power*, Hutchinson.

BRIDGES, LORD (1964), *The Treasury*, Allen and Unwin.

CLAPHAM, SIR JOHN (reprinted 1964), *The Bank of England—A History* (2 vols), Cambridge University Press.

CLAY, SIR HENRY (1957), *Lord Norman*, Macmillan.

COBBOLD, LORD (1962), *Some Thoughts on Central Banking*, Athlone Press.

DAY, A. C. L., 'The Organisation and Status of the Bank of England', *Public Administration*, xxxviii (1960), 67-72.

DAY, A. C. L., 'The Bank of England in the Modern State', *Public Administration*, xxxix (1961), 15-26.

DODWELL, D. W. (1934), *Treasuries and Central Banks*, P. S. King and Son.

HAWTRY, R. G. (1938), *A Century of Bank Rate*, Longmans Green.

SAYERS, R. S. (1964, 6th edition), *Modern Banking*, Clarendon Press.

SAYERS, R. S. (1957), *Central Banking After Bagehot*, Clarendon Press.

THORNEYCROFT, PETER, *et al.* (1960), *Not Unanimous*, Institute of Economic Affairs.

F. Other Works

BLAKE, ROBERT (1955), *The Unknown Prime Minister*, Eyre and Spottiswoode.

FRIEDRICH, CARL J. (editor) (1958), *Authority* (Nomos 1), Cambridge Mass.: Harvard University Press.

GAUS, J. M. (1947), *Reflections on Public Administration*, Alabama: University of Alabama Press.

KELLY, SIR DAVID (1952), *The Ruling Few*, Hollis and Carter.